GW01336955

Golf EQ

The Game Between Shots

DR. IZZY JUSTICE

iUniverse

GOLF EQ
The Game Between Shots

Copyright © 2017 Dr. Izzy Justice.

All rights reserved. No part of this book may be used or reproduced by any means, graphic, electronic, or mechanical, including photocopying, recording, taping or by any information storage retrieval system without the written permission of the author except in the case of brief quotations embodied in critical articles and reviews.

iUniverse books may be ordered through booksellers or by contacting:

iUniverse
1663 Liberty Drive
Bloomington, IN 47403
www.iuniverse.com
1-800-Authors (1-800-288-4677)

Because of the dynamic nature of the Internet, any web addresses or links contained in this book may have changed since publication and may no longer be valid. The views expressed in this work are solely those of the author and do not necessarily reflect the views of the publisher, and the publisher hereby disclaims any responsibility for them.

Any people depicted in stock imagery provided by Thinkstock are models, and such images are being used for illustrative purposes only. Certain stock imagery © Thinkstock.

ISBN: 978-1-5320-1323-2 (sc)
ISBN: 978-1-5320-1324-9 (hc)
ISBN: 978-1-5320-1322-5 (e)

Library of Congress Control Number: 2016920992

Print information available on the last page.

iUniverse rev. date: 12/22/2016

Dedication

To Stephanie, Lexi, Hunter and my
eternal mentor, Gary Mason.

Acknowledgments

This book would not be possible without the input of professional golfer and EQ certified coach, David Sanchez, who provided invaluable research and insight. I am also grateful to my editor, Anjum Khan.

Contents

Foreword xi
Introduction xiii
Chapter 1 1
      Why Train in EQ? 3
Chapter 2 17
      Neuroscience of a Golfer 18
Chapter 3 46
      Art and Science of Learning 47
Chapter 4 68
      Happiness & Focus 69
Chapter 5 89
      Phases of Golf 90
Chapter 6 104
      Warm Up 105
Chapter 7 115
      18 Holes of Competition 116
Chapter 8 131
      Post-Round 132
Chapter 9 143
      Caddying 144
Chapter 10 150
      Life Balance 151

Foreword

Having played golf my entire life all over the world, I can speak to not only how much fun this game is, but also to how challenging it is. No doubt golf is a puzzle without an answer. Frankly, the hardest part about golf is to realize it is a game of mistakes. Many things are not going to go the way you want, like in life. And that's one reason we love golf so much because it is such a true microcosm of life. You can hit a great shot and it can land in a bad lie. You can miss a 3-foot putt for reasons that are inexplicable. You can make some terrible decisions on the golf course that afterwards look even worse.

In an average round of golf that takes about 4 ½ hours, you are actually only hitting the ball less than 15 minutes of that time. The rest of the time you are thinking and feeling. Golf is as much a mental and emotional game as it is skills related. We have known this forever, but we do not always know how to prepare for it the way we can easily go practice bunker play, or putting, or iron play...until now.

Dr. Izzy Justice has written a book that does just that. It is filled with neuroscience – the study of how the brain makes decisions – and with templates in the book that you have to fill out to build your own strategy. Golf is also emotional. One shot makes you feel good as fast as a bad shot can make you feel bad. Dr. Justice gives us a language and framework to process emotions in golf and make better decisions so we can enjoy this beautiful game a little bit more.

Gary Player
World Golf Hall of Fame
9-Time Major Winner
165 Professional Victories over 5 decades

Introduction

As a sports neuropsychologist, I have worked with professional athletes, coaches, teams in many sports, as well as with business professionals for almost three decades specializing in Emotional Intelligence (EQ). I have found a profound deficiency in the emotional literacy of people in general whereby most folks do not even have a language to process emotions. Athletes in particular, who are gifted physically in their sport, are even more deficient because of the deep introspection often required to learn and grow one's EQ, that often takes away from the physical training of their sport. As a single-digit handicapper myself, I am proud to share in this book very practical information that will allow you to get the best out of yourself. Each chapter will begin with a blog post that I write weekly, in which I also include tips to build EQ.

Golf is played in over 200 countries. There are over 34,000 golf courses in the world. The U.S. has the most, with over 15,000. In 2005, player participation in the U.S. was at its peak, with roughly 30 million players. Shortly after that, numbers dropped steeply to around 24 million. In the last four years, the numbers have increased and are holding steady at around 25 million players.

There are 1289 men's college golf programs and 939 women's programs. Division One programs have the highest number of teams from both sexes, with 299 men's and 262 women's programs. For these Division One programs, over 9 million dollars are given out in scholarships combined.

In the last nine years, golf equipment sales in the U.S. topped out at 3.72 billion dollars in 2007, and bottomed out to 2.92 billion dollars in 2009. It increased each of the next four years, reaching 3.67 billion dollars in 2013 before falling slightly in 2014 and 2015. The top five world golf markets are: (i) U.S., (ii) Japan, (iii) South Korea, (iv) U.K., and (v) Canada. These five markets represent 80% of total equipment sales. The U.S. and Japan control over 65% of the world market. In 2015, golf generated 8.7 billion dollars globally.

The two governing bodies are the United States Golf Association (USGA) and the R&A. The USGA was founded in 1894 and is the governing body in the U.S. and Mexico only. The R&A was originally founded in 1754 as the *Society of St. Andrews Golfers* (in Scotland), and it governs the rest of the world.

One can discern from all these hard statistics that golf is a lucrative and global sport, and growing at the junior levels at an unprecedented rate. What these facts do not show is the spirit and soul of golf.

Golf is as much a sport as it is a social and business enterprise. There are vast housing developments built around golf courses so that homes can have views of fairways, greens, flowers and ponds. There are social events, like Member-Guest tournaments, that usually are the annual highlight for most clubs. Golfers take golf trips around the country and world to build friendships and take a break from the hustle and bustle of work and family life. Vacations are planned around golf destinations that also cater to non-golfers with amenities like a spa.

A ton of business is also conducted on the golf course. Corporate outings and business dealings are a norm as the change in scenery from office space is often a welcome difference, not to mention an emotionally-disarming environment.

There is the relaxation and physical health component that most retirees cherish. It feels great to get out of the house, and go out with little physical stress and walk on fairways. Many find it therapeutic as the social interaction with friends in an outdoor setting just feels good.

It can be easy to forget, given all these benefits of the game of golf, that it is a sport requiring skills that have measurable outcomes. Golf, for all practical purposes, is an endurance sport. An average round of golf for 18 holes lasts about 4.5 hours. That's about the same time it takes on average to complete a full marathon of 26.2 miles, or just an hour less than a half ironman event of 1.2 miles of swimming, 56 miles of riding a bike, and 13.1 miles of running.

What makes golf the ultimate endurance test is that it is quite practically 93% mental and 7% physical. How so? It takes anywhere between 5 and 15 seconds to actually hit a golf shot. That is, to take a club back and strike the ball physically. With an average score of 85 shots for 18 holes, that is less than 20 minutes of physical activity. This means that in a 4.5 hour round, 4.1 hours are spent on non-physical activity that very few golfers have any plan for. **It begs the question of why almost 100% of time training for golf is spent on the physical activity - yet almost no time is spent on the game of golf between shots.**

This book is largely about managing that 93% of golf. It is about having a plan to play golf with the best chance of being fully ready (mentally, emotionally and physically) to hit the next shot to the best of your ability, whatever that ability is.

The central premise of this book is that golf is as much an emotional endurance test as it is a golf skill test.

If you do not believe this, then this book will be of little value to you. If you do, then the next logical question should be: What do I do to prepare for the emotional endurance test?

In this book, I will introduce you to a sequence of mental and emotional preparation, before, during and after a round as well as for practice. You will be introduced to a new mental and emotional language similar to the physical language of golf. In the latter, golfers know what a bunker is, what fairways, greens or rough are, and what a putter is versus an iron or a driver or wedge. These are all words that form a language that allow you to understand the physical game of golf ... for that mere 3% of your round.

In addition to a new language, you will build your own personal game plan. No two human beings are the same mentally and emotionally, so the plan for each person will be different and has to accommodate the emotional fluctuations of both life and golf, where highs and lows can impact so much of decision-making.

During a round of golf, the sheer volume of monologues that occur is quite unprecedented. Each monologue, that self-talk, after almost every shot, is a natural human response to the stimuli of the ever-changing environment. Whether it is the tee box, the wind, the rain, the heat, the playing partner, the lie, the pin position, the inconsistent greens, bunkers, or fairways, or whatever myriad of unique circumstances that literally each shot presents itself, the environment in golf is constantly changing and challenging. Compound this with the competitive environment of whoever you are playing with or against, your expectations or handicap, no teammates or coaches to help you, as well as the myriad of things that can go wrong, I am talking about a totally unique environment that will challenge your emotions to the core.

These emotions, both good and not so good ones, will dictate the tone and content of the monologues and critical subsequent decision-making. In Chapter 1, I will share several stories that almost all golfers will be able to relate to where they themselves got in their own way, failed to execute their strategy for the physical game, and underperformed.

Yet despite powerful personal stories of underperformance and many more well-documented ones from professional golfers, the average golfer still spends almost zero time training his or her emotions and thoughts. I researched dozens of golf training programs and videos and found very few that had budgeted time for this kind of training.

As a neuro-sports psychologist, one of the first questions I ask any golfer who comes to me is: What is the most difficult shot in golf? The most common answers I get are the first tee shot or a 40-yard bunker shot, or a few will say the next shot. **It is my absolute contention that the most difficult shot in golf is the one right after a bad one.** Why? As I will explain in Chapter 2, right after a bad shot, the emotional temperature is so high that cognitive decision-making is neurologically compromised, leading to a very low probability that you can either make the right next decision or physically execute that next shot to the best of your ability.

This is the reason to write this book. I believe that most golfers are grossly under training in an area that has the potential to be a game-changer in performance. The inexplicable reason, I believe, that very established golf coaches and very intelligent and hard-working golfers are under training in this area is simply because they do not know how to do it. If it is done, it is done anecdotally, not with any scientific basis, nor with an accommodation for the unique emotional condition of each human being.

This book is not about swinging the golf club correctly, putting correcting, getting more distance or the short game, nor is it about any equipment. There are plenty of resources for these dimensions of the sport that are readily available. Golfers are notorious for buying anything that they believe will make them perform better, but there is no off-the-shelve equipment for our emotions that can be purchased. **This is a personal endeavor.**

This book brings decades of experience and neuroscience. I hope this book will be an invaluable asset to your practice and round of golf. I will start the book with real-life stories and quickly proceed to why it is so important to master the art of learning from your mistakes in the golf. Then I will provide you with detailed and easily understandable neuroscience of how the human body works; what emotions are and how they are created; how to recognize, label and manage them during practice, pre-round anxieties, and each situation in your round. There will also be a chapter on how to be an effective caddie – whether as a professional caddie or a parent or coach. Each chapter will have both EQ and practical tips. Finally, I will explore happiness and life-balance: two areas that I believe are also under trained with roots in EQ.

The goal is to not just give you tips to be a better golfer, but to help you understand why that tip will work for your body from a neuroscience perspective. The explicit intention is that you fully understand why these tips work so you can make adjustments as warranted instead of just doing things and hoping they work. This combination of knowledge is guaranteed to help you with your goals, and almost surely, with your personal journey of growth as well.

Essentially, two books are being provided to you: one that I wrote, and the other written by you in the spaces provided in this book. **Thus, if you do all of the written exercises suggested, you will have a second book written by you, and for you. Either or both of these books can be read many times over during your season.**

Emotional endurance and mental strength are not just a part of golf, but also a part of life. It can be argued that life itself is an emotional endurance test. And this may be what makes golf so popular, as you can draw parallels between training for and playing a round, and your own life's journey. It is possible to feel many highs and lows and everything in between in a round of golf – a microcosm of life. I hope that the reader-interactive format will impact both your physical and emotional endurance to get you to perform to the best of your ability when it counts the most.

Chapter 1

One of the mentors who works for me reached out to me over the weekend. He had been struck by a question his mentee had posted and wanted my input prior to responding. His mentee told him that in some of the most popular books and literature, **there seems to be universal agreement that negative experiences and the resulting negative emotions are either to be avoided or to be ignored.** *The widespread message seems to be to not to dwell on negativity and instead leverage the power of "positive energy" and "positive thinking."*

I am all for a positive attitude. I mean, who wants to work or live with someone who sees the proverbial glass half empty all the time? What good could possibly come from an athlete saying "I am going to fail" in the middle of his or her performance? In this context, yes, I agree that a positive attitude is very good, healthy, and in most cases, contagious.

But I gathered from this mentor that this notion was being extrapolated into an unrealistic territory — in the context of life, in general. It is unrealistic for positivity to be applied so broadly. For one thing, **negative experiences are a natural part of life** *… they will occur whether you want them to or not. When I speak, I often ask my audience to raise their hands if they wake up every morning and hope for something negative to happen. No hands go up. I then ask them to raise their hands if something bad happens anyway … and all the hands go up. So negative experiences are going to happen.*

In addition, **negative emotions are necessary for positive ones to exist.** *If you've never been sad, it is quite possible you've never been truly* happy either. *If you've ever had a great day or a great experience, it is likely because you can juxtapose that to previous days or previous experiences that perhaps were not so good. In other words, it is easy to read popular literature (mostly non-scientific) and begin to take matters out of context.*

While I am not suggesting we proactively seek negative experiences, I am suggesting that we seek new and challenging experiences where the likelihood of failure is possible. I am suggesting that in lieu of nonchalantly brushing off negative experiences for fear of "being too negative" or "dwelling on the negative" that we **embrace our negative experiences***. In my third book (*Is Today The Day*?) I interviewed dozens of Stage IV cancer patients. Almost all told me that they learned more from their mistakes in life than their successes and wished they had taken more risks. To learn from mistakes, and to figure out ways to make yourself and the world better as a result, is truly one of life's grandest opportunities. The rewards are incalculable and the resultant emotions are just priceless.*

My point this week is to not mistake a positive attitude for avoiding learning from negative experiences. Whatever you feel is right. If you're sad, and asked, "How are you?" — concede that you are sad ... with the expectation that it is an effort to make yourself better. Responding to the previous question with "Doing just great! How about you?" is not only deceiving and disingenuous, it is not necessary. I urge my readers to not throw the gift of negative experiences away. They happen every day whether we want them to or not. By simply questioning and dialoguing, we can probably find ways to make ourselves, others, and life better. **This is the power of emotions***.*

https://izzyjustice.wordpress.com/2009/07/06/negative-experiences-and-emotions/

Why Train in EQ?

So why invest in learning about Emotional Intelligence (EQ)? I recognize that you are already spending hours on the range, on the putting green, in the short-game area playing with 14 different clubs each of which can hit a variety of shots depending on grip, swing, force of hit, and so on. There is a lot to practice in the physical game of golf and shots to have. There are also all the equipment changes that come out every year from clubs to grips to balls and so much more. So why add yet one more dimension to your practice plan? Perhaps the best way to establish the case for this is to review several examples of what happens all the time in golf and other sports. Below are actual stories by professionals and amateurs alike. I had literally hundreds to choose from, but selected just a few that underscore the fact the mishaps are virtually guaranteed to occur in golf, and it is your emotional response to them that can be the difference between underperforming and recovering to overachieve.

"I think maybe I hit only one perfect shot a round." –Jack Nicklaus

- In the 1989 Masters, Scott Hoch had a one shot lead with two holes to go. As he walked to the 17th tee, he said he started thinking about winning the tournament for the first time. He hit his drive into the 15th fairway, from where he said he made a mental mistake by trying to hit his second shot all the way back to the flag, instead of leaving it underneath the hole like he knew he should have. He hit it over the green and missed a short putt for par. He ended up in a playoff with Nick Faldo. On the first hole of the playoff, #10, Hoch hit a perfect drive and second shot in the middle of the green, while Faldo hit it in a greenside bunker and made bogey. Hoch had to two-putt an uphill 20-footer for the win. He ran his first putt two and a half feet past the hole and had a downhill left to right breaking putt for the win. He recalled that on the 17th hole, he had backed off his short par putt, which he missed. On the playoff hole, he said that he wanted to hit the breaking putt firmly, so as to eliminate most of the break, but he wasn't comfortable over the ball and knew that he was aiming too far to the left for the speed he wanted to hit the putt with. He said that he didn't want to back off again, because of what happened on 17, so he continued on. Everything seemed to be going too fast. He ultimately hit the putt too hard for where he was aiming and missed the putt that would have won him the tournament. He then lost the playoff on the next hole.

Analysis: The emotional anxiety of potentially winning led him to hit his shot on 15 farther. The emotional memory of the putt on 17th compromised his ability to hit the putt harder on the playoff hole. High negative emotions redirected his neuropathways (thinking routes in the brain) so everything appears faster as fewer options are explored. **The challenge was not physical, it was emotional.**

> In the 1970 British Open at St. Andrews, Doug Sanders had a two foot putt on the 18th green to beat Jack Nicklaus by a shot. Sanders said that over the final three holes, he was already thinking that he had won the tournament and how great it was. On his two-footer on 18, Sanders took an inordinately long amount of time over the ball. Before he took the putter back, he was distracted by what he thought was a small pebble between his ball and the hole. He bent down to pick it up, only to realize that it was just a piece of discolored grass. Instead of going through his normal routine again, he went straight back to his stance over the ball. He said he could hear people in the gallery laughing and he thought to himself, "I'll teach them to laugh at me" instead of thinking about his putt, which he ended up missing. He lost a playoff to Nicklaus the next day and never won a single major championship.

Analysis: Hitting a two-foot putt was not the issue. Allowing his focus to wonder was. **The challenge was not physical, it was emotional.**

➢ In the 1961 Masters, Arnold Palmer was leading Gary Player by one shot when he hit his drive to the middle of the fairway on 18. It was going to be his third Masters in four years. His good friend, George Low, was in the gallery at the spot of his 2nd shot and congratulated him on his victory. Palmer proceeded to hit his shot into the greenside bunker and make a double bogey to lose to Player by a shot. In many interviews Palmer has given since regarding that loss, he regrets how his emotions got the better of him with the congratulatory comment.

Analysis: Even for the most talented and skilled golfers, vulnerability to unwelcome emotions and thoughts is high. The racing thoughts in his head over-powered the ability to hit the desired shot. **The challenge was not physical, it was emotional.**

➢ In the 1999 British Open at Carnoustie, Jean Van de Velde held a three-shot lead on the 18th tee. Knowing that he only needed a double bogey to win, Van de Velde hit a driver off the tee instead of a 3-wood or even a long iron for safety. He hit it so far to the right that he luckily avoided the water hazard to the right of the fairway and ended up on the 17th hole. When the camera man zoomed in on his face after the tee shot, Van de Velde put his hand over the lens in embarrassment. After the fortunate break off the tee, he merely needed to pitch the ball back to the fairway and then play to the green from there. He later said that he didn't want to win that way, by pitching back to the fairway, and instead wanted to win with a flare by hitting a 2-iron over the hazard in front of the green. His 2-iron flew into the grandstand to the right of the green, ricocheted off a metal pole, hopped off the rock wall of the hazard, and buried itself in a miserable lie in the waist high rough, still not over the water yet. Again, instead of pitching the ball sideways, he tried to go over the hazard, but didn't hit it hard enough and hit it right in the middle of the water. After a drop, a pitch that found the front bunker, and a bunker shot, he ended up having to make a 7-footer for triple bogey just to get into a three man playoff, which he eventually lost.

Analysis: Pitching the ball back in play was the right "cognitive" decision with the lead he had. His emotional desire to look heroic in victory trumped an otherwise simple decision. **The challenge was not physical, it was emotional.**

> In the 2016 Masters, Ernie Els was playing his first hole of the first round. After missing the green and chipping up to three feet, Els experienced one of the worst cases of the yips that have ever been seen. Just the previous week in Houston, he had led the field in putting from inside of 10 feet. His stroke on the first green was so shaky and violent that he never even came close to hitting the hole on his 3-footer. He did the same thing on the comeback attempt from two feet and ended up missing three more times from less than three feet. He ended up six-putting the hole for a score of nine, and ultimately missed the cut. He admitted after the round that his game coming into the week was very sharp and he put a lot of pressure on himself to win a tournament that he desperately wanted to win in the late stages of his career.

Analysis: With each miss, it was less about a two-foot putt and more about the emotion of failure which diluted his focus on a routine putt. **The challenge was not physical, it was emotional.**

> At the second stage of the 2012 PGA Tour Qualifying Tournament, a mini-tour player had finally gotten off to a solid start at the stage that had been his stumbling block to getting back out onto a major tour. This was the last year in which players could play their way straight onto the PGA Tour, but still with the consolation prize of assuring membership on the Web.com Tour. Through two rounds, he was nine under

par and had only made a single bogey. As he sat in the hotel room that evening, his mind started thinking ahead to how great it would be to at least get back out on the Web.com Tour, where he hadn't played since 2007. He was well inside the cut number and playing nearly flawlessly, so he was essentially planning his schedule out for the next year. He was paired with two high profile players in the 3rd round and felt like his brain was in a cloud all day. He was caught up in comparing his game to theirs and began hitting poor shot after poor shot. He shot 74 in the third round to put himself on the cut line. He was again paired with two notable players in the last round, and was again playing in a mental fog. He shot 75 in the final round to miss advancing.

Analysis: **There are three competitors in golf in this order: (i) You, (ii) the course, and (ii) other golfers.** The emotion playing with two better-known players reversed the order of importance and focus. **The challenge was not physical, it was emotional.**

> In the 1991 Ryder Cup at the Ocean Course at Kiawah Island, Mark Calcevecchia was playing against Colin Montgomery in the Sunday singles matches. Calcevecchia was four up with four to play and knew that even a half point either way could win or lose the Cup. Montgomery won the 15th and 16th holes, but hit his tee shot in the water on the par 3 17th. Needing only to hit the ball on dry land, Calcevecchia topped his tee shot into the water. After both dropped and played to the green, Calcevecchia needed a two-footer for a double bogey that would tie the hole and win the match. He missed the putt and lost the 18th hole as well to end up halving the match. After suffering what appeared to be a panic attack in the minutes following the match, Calcevecchia said that he had suddenly felt the entire weight of winning the Ryder Cup for his teammates when he was '4 up with 4 to play' and it became too big for him.

Analysis: The "weight" he is talking about is nothing more than the extreme emotional condition of that moment. The mistake was not feeling that, but rather not knowing how to deal with it. **The challenge was not physical, it was emotional.**

> ➤ A junior golfer had an AJGA tournament where several college coaches would be in attendance. She had been playing very well and had a great practice before the round. To her surprise, when she walked up to the first tee, virtually all the coaches were there even though several groups had already started before her. She had played in front of people before, but she said she had never felt so many eyes on her and became aware that every single thing she did on that tee box would be analyzed. She proceeded to block her shot out of bounds and never recovered. The rest of the round she was more anxious to finish and get out than to try to recover and salvage a decent score.

Analysis: Her issue on the tee box had nothing to do with all the practice she had done on her physical game. She told me later she never practiced for a moment like that and had no idea how to process all that stimuli in her head. **The challenge was not physical, it was emotional.**

> ➤ In the 1996 Masters, Greg Norman held a six-shot lead going into the last round. The Masters was always the tournament that he wanted to win the most, but it was also where he had suffered the most crushing defeats of his career in years past. He had played flawlessly in the first round, tying the course and major championship record of 63. His play had become more ragged over the next two rounds, but most analysts were still practically conceding him the tournament with 18 holes to go. In an interview almost 20 years later, Norman admitted that when he woke up Sunday morning, he could sense that he was "off". He said that he was struggling with an off the course issue that was at the verge of boiling over, yet he never told anyone about it. On the range before the round, he

admitted that he was panicking, despite his coach and caddie both telling him his swing looked perfect. On the course, he opened with a bogey and made mistake after mistake, eventually shooting 78 and losing by five shots to Nick Faldo.

Analysis: We are human beings with one brain. There is no way to compartmentalize personal life from golf as it is the same brain that houses all experiences and memories. Personal life has arguably the largest emotional impact on a golfer because golf is a non-reactive (unlike say basketball or tennis) sport where most of the time (93%) is not on the physical game. **The challenge was not physical, it was emotional.**

➢ In the 2016 Masters, Jordan Spieth was attempting to become the fourth player in history to win back to back tournaments, as well as his 3rd major championship. During the final round, Spieth made four consecutive birdies from holes 6-9 to open up a five-shot lead with nine holes to play. After playing his most solid nine holes of the tournament, Spieth later said that he started the back nine just trying to make pars to protect his lead. He began to hit poor shot after poor shot and made two bogeys in a row before hitting his tee shot in the water on number 12. After taking his drop, he proceeded to chunk his third shot into the water again and made a quadruple bogey. He ultimately lost the tournament by three shots. When later asked what his thinking was during those shots in the water, he said, "I don't know what I was thinking. It was a tough 30 minutes that I hope I never experience again."

Analysis: "Not being able to think clearly" is the sure sign that emotions have taken over, not that you cannot think. Managing emotions well is determined by how quickly you can think clearly again after a bad shot. **The challenge was not physical, it was emotional.**

➢ In 2014, a new reality show came out called, *The Short Game*. The show documented a group of junior golfers, ages

7-9, and their parents, as they prepared for and competed in tournaments around the country. In most of the cases, a parent would caddie for the child during the competition and would very often harshly criticize and yell at the child after he or she made the first mistake of the round. This more often than not would trigger a tailspin of worse shots by the child and even harsher criticism from the parent, leaving the child in tears before the round was even over. The children in those situations never showed any signs of improvement during the season and often appeared to resent the game as well.

Analysis: Experiences are stories told using words in monologues in our minds. Each carries an emotional value especially from people of value in our lives. For kids, and young adults, golf is mostly emotional as what it means to self- esteem and acceptance by others matters more. **The challenge was not physical, it was emotional.**

Clearly, there are hundreds more of these kinds of stories that can be shared. And it is not just in golf.

Other Sports

Athletes from all sports experience similar mishaps, setbacks, and losses that are not attributable to the athlete's physical or technical skills. What must be noted in these other sports and athletes is that the common thread is how all athletes are, first, human beings built with the same physiology and neuroscience, and exhibiting the same emotional responses as golfers.

> ➢ A basketball player practices free throws thousands of times and makes all of them, yet something is different when the free throw has to be made with one second to go and the game is on the line. What is different? Is it the size of the basketball? The size of the rim? The distance to the basket? Did the basketball player suddenly lose weight or get shorter or lose 20 IQ points?

No, of course not. What is different is the pressure of the situation – the emotions of the situation. This is not physical, it is emotional.

- At an Ironman event, a pro athlete was leading the race until about mile 16 of the run when another pro athlete passed him. He had led the entire race and was shocked to get caught. So disheartened by this, he decided to try to keep up with the new leader and go faster than he knew he could. Intellectually, he knew that he could not keep up the faster pace this late in the race but chose to ignore this, and push himself even harder. By mile 22, he was spent and instead of a certain 2nd place finish, he ended up 12th. After the race, he was visibly upset. He just could not understand why he reacted the way he did when he got passed, why he abandoned his race strategy and how he let his emotions at the time he got passed cause him to ignore his training, and instead adopt a totally unrealistic running pace. He clearly underperformed and it had little to do with his physical skills.

- A NASCAR driver and his crew chief tell me that the race is called and raced differently in the first 200 laps versus the last 50 laps. The difference between the winner and the next 10 drivers is literally seconds, so the last 50 laps are critical for finishing position. But the track is the same as it was in the first 200 laps. What is different is the pressure of those last laps where critical decisions are made. Those last laps are no longer about cars and all about the decisions the driver and crew chief make. It is not about the equipment, but the emotions of the situation.

- A professional tennis player tells me the difference between the first four sets and the fifth set is just one thing: mental strength. She says it almost ceases to be about tennis, and whoever can remain calm in the moment of pressure and execute the shots they know they have hit thousands of times before in the fifth set almost always wins. What is the difference between the sets? What is different is the pressure of the situation – the emotions of the situation.

> ➢ The New York Knicks had a 105-99 lead with just 18.7 seconds left before Indiana Pacers' guard, Reggie Miller, sent them falling into one of the most stunning end-game collapses in NBA history by scoring eight points in nine mind-blowing seconds. Miller began by hitting a 3-pointer. Then he stole the ensuing inbounds pass and dashed back out to the 3-point line, where he wheeled and drained another 3 to tie the game at 105. "We were shell-shocked, we were numb," Knicks forward, Anthony Mason, remembered years later. "We became totally disoriented." The Knicks still had a few more chances to win, but John Starks missed two free throws and Knicks center, Patrick Ewing, missed a 10-footer before Miller was fouled on the rebound. He made both free throws to give the Pacers a shocking 107-105 win, and then he ran off the Madison Square Garden floor yelling, "Choke artists!" The Pacers went on to win the series in seven games.
> -- *Johnette Howard*

Terms like "shell-shocked" and "disoriented" used by the Knicks and so many other athletes in all sports to describe how they felt are lay terms, in effect conceding that "something" happened to them that they cannot explain. For any athlete, golfer or any sport, there should be no part of your performance that you should not be prepared for, much less not be able to explain.

It should be noted that there is a fundamental difference between these kinds of stories of underperformance and others where athletes underperform because of physical reasons. If you have a strained back, it is going to be tough to hit the shots you know you can hit no matter how much emotional strength you have. When something irreparable happens to your body, no amount of EQ can compensate for that. Similarly, if you do not have the skill to do something in practice, then no amount of mental strength can create that skill on the golf course. If you do not have a high draw in your repertoire and never hit that shot successfully on the range, you simply can't "will" yourself to do it.

As a neuro-sports psychologist, I have found that disappointment and frustration does not come from failing to execute on something never done before. It comes from **the true definition of underperformance which is the inability to execute on the very things you have done many times before, but not when in matters most: during game-time**. It is the examples given above that are much harder to swallow because you feel it was something 'mental' and the root cause of your poor reaction is still inexplicably a mystery to you. In these underperforming situations, you feel like you 'lost' control and let something derail you. You feel like you beat yourself. This is where EQ can make a tremendous difference.

"What separates great players from the good ones is not so much ability as brain power and emotional equilibrium." -Arnold Palmer

So Why Train EQ?

As described, rounds of golf are littered with these stories of self-inflicted wounds where the mind chose to make poor decisions in the heat of battle during 'game time', and in many cases, decisions that were contrary to what they and their coaches had already agreed on during training. Why did their minds deviate from their strategy? Why did they react in a manner where in hindsight, and with a much clearer mind, they would have all made different and better decisions? What is it about golfers' emotions during anxiety situations that shut down very logical decision-making, decisions that they can make on any other day without blinking an eye? What could they have done during practice to prepare them for the 'heat of the battle' scenarios?

In all sports, if athletes are able to maintain composure, access their training memories, and simply perform as they have trained, their chances of being successful go up significantly. This is obvious. How to do it is not so obvious. *This is why we train EQ.* We prepare ourselves to stay focused and positive in the midst of mishaps and distractions so that we can perform our best - be it on the golf course or in everyday experiences.

The reality is that golf is a game of mishaps.

Since golf is full of mishaps, it is therefore a game of emotional strength. This is a learnable skill, like any other, and is required 93% of the time you are playing golf. This fundamental shift in reframing how you view and play golf is the first step in building your Golf EQ.

We define emotional strength as the amount of time it takes to convert a negative thought to a positive one.

My contention is that not only can these mishaps be managed differently during a round, but in fact, you can effectively train for them and increase your EQ. It is impossible to predict what is going to go wrong and when it will happen, but suffice it to say, in all likelihood something will happen that will cause anxiety just before or during your round. This we can all agree on. And if you concede this, then, in order to perform at your best on the day and hit a shot that counts, your practice must prepare you to manage your emotions and thoughts. A plan that incorporates EQ training will help you manage the unpredictable but certain-to-occur anxiety-inducing experiences and your response to it. As noted in the introduction, if you are going to spend so much time and money desperately searching for a perfect swing and shot, why not spend just a few minutes a day to grow your EQ and remain positive and focused in the throes of situations that are beyond your control? No one wishes for chaos of any kind during a round, but **a positive recovery from a bad situation can actually**

be incredibly motivating and powerful to spur you on to an even better performance.

"Competitive golf is played mainly on a five-and-a-half inch court, the space between your ears." -Bobby Jones

Please take a few moments to write down in your own words an experience where you underperformed in a round, similar to the stories shared earlier in this chapter. In subsequent chapters, as tips are shared, you will be asked to come back to this story and personalize your learning. By writing down your own personal experiences, your own emotions and presence in the experience will make the learning and subsequent growth a much richer endeavor. As you write your story, try to describe yourself emotionally, mentally, and physically, as well as describe the situation you were in as graphically as you can.

Note that a mishap is not just a situation where something has gone terribly wrong, like the stories described earlier, but mishaps can be anything where you have lost your focus and as a result, deviated from your capabilities and underperformed.

Exercise:

My Personal Story of Under-Performing

Top 3 Ideas
I learned from this chapter
1.
2.
3.
3 Action Steps
I will take immediately to incorporate the above learning into my practice and competitive rounds
1.
2.
3.

Chapter Summary

1. Mishaps are bound to occur on every round. They happen to all golfers – professional and amateurs.
2. When mishaps happen, our emotions are tested. This emotional test is what most golfers need to train for also.
3. When your emotional reaction to a mishap is poor, your decision-making is compromised and you underperform.

Chapter 2

*I shared the TED video (*http://www.ted.com/talks/jinsop_lee_design_for_all_5_senses.html*) on the 5 senses last week even though I have blogged about the 5 senses in the past. I have been arguing for many years how underutilized our senses are, mostly because we simply have been using them from the time we were born but never been actually trained to optimize them or to comprehend the extent of their relevance to our emotions and the substantive experiences of our lives. The video and I both hold that the greater all 5 senses are engaged, the more meaningful an experience is and the higher the probability that it will be retained in our memory.*

The implications of this are not just for our personal lives. Think of all the day-to-day activities you perform, meetings you have, calls you make, emails you write, and home activities you perform with your family. Working professionals constantly have an audience and if you are in a position where you want that audience, whether it is a spouse or a business customer, to remember you, then an approach that proactively appeals to the audience's 5 senses will likely get you there.

I have blogged about office spaces previously and how uninspiring most of them are. What makes them boring is their lack of appeal to any of the senses. As a leader, home or work, you want the eyes of the people around you to fall, intentionally or unintentionally, on inspiring images. You want them to hear sounds of collaboration and positive dialogues. You want them to feel like it is a safe place worth taking risks. And so on and so forth.

Take a walk into your home, your personal office at work and your entire office floor or building. Just walk through it. Take inventory of what you see, hear, feel, smell and touch. Is any of it inspiring to you? If so, great. If not, then how can you expect it to be for everyone else? Take inventory of your meetings, emails, and all other activities in the same way. Are they inspiring to you? Do they make you want to bring out your best? So, what can you do? Draw a graph just as in the TED video and plot the graph for each activity you are engaged in. Think of ways you can enhance all the experiences by simply increasing the low-utilized senses in the activities. I assure you that you will be astonished at how much more exciting life can suddenly become.

https://izzyjustice.wordpress.com/2013/09/08/5-sense-ii/

Neuroscience of a Golfer

It is critical that you understand how your body works physiologically. Your body is the ultimate equipment in your round. If you can shell out thousands of dollars on equipment like your clubs, and spend years perfecting the golf swing, then consider spending quality time on understanding your body as a piece of equipment that you need to appreciate with the same amount of passion and detail. Unlike the 14 clubs you are playing with, however, your body (emotions and thoughts) is constantly changing, which makes understanding it even more important. Imagine playing with 14 clubs that change in shaft or grip or lie angle after each shot? That would be crazy and a recipe for disaster. Yet, that is exactly what is happening to your emotions after each shot – they are constantly changing. **The most important equipment that you use on every shot, your body, is constantly changing!**

When a golfer comes to see me, one of the first questions I ask him or her is to describe his or her favorite club to me. If it is a driver, the golfer will describe in infinite detail the shaft length, flex, club head size and materials, grip, and so much more. After the detailed description, I pause and then ask for a description of his or her brain. I get the same reaction you just had. "Huh?"

If all the decisions are made in only one part of your body—and that's your brain—then of all the tools and skills to master, knowing your brain and how it works is the singular most important skill all golfers, amateurs and professionals alike, should invest in.

How many decisions do you have to make in a round of golf? Please take a few moments to do the following exercise.

Exercise: Decisions made in a round of golf

Make a list of most common cognitive decisions you have to make in a round of golf

1. _____

2. _____

3. _____

4. _____

5. _____

6. _____

7. _____

8. _____

9. _____

10. _____

There are probably another 10 you can easily come up with. So you can see, there are a ton of decisions to be made in a round of golf and they are all made in and by only one part of your body: your brain.

Superior Performance

The ultimate goal for you is to perform at your best on the course when it matters. Not on the range and not during practice rounds, but when it matters most: during game time - when every shot really counts. Period. Once you are physically ready (training), and as discussed in many examples in Chapter 1, good and timely decision-making, which only occurs in the brain (not in your grip, your elbows, your hips or spine angle) is at the heart of optimal performance, where you are able to perform these physical skills. Decision-making, therefore, is the centerpiece to optimal performance since without it, you are guaranteed to underperform.

This begins the understanding of how decisions are made. There is a neurological sequence with how all decisions are made. Let us start with the end result and work backwards.

As shown below, superior performance is the end game with good decision-making at the center of it.

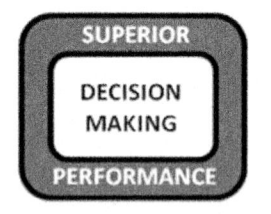

Figure 1. Superior Performance

Competency

The way that you know you are making good decisions during a round is directly related to your ability to execute your physical abilities, or competencies. Competencies or skills are the things we know how to do because of how we have trained. They are specific skills and abilities, such as the mechanics of your golf swing or your shot game. Golfers spend an enormous amount of time here. In other words, good training and technique play a big part in decision-making and subsequent performance. But most of you already know this.

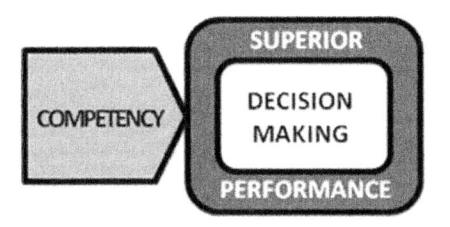

Figure 2. Competency

Behavior

Preceding our competencies and skills, are our behaviors. See below for the sequence of understanding how good decisions are made.

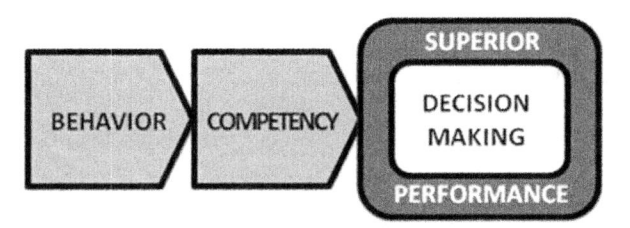

Figure 3. Behavior

Behaviors are essentially the framework of how we show our thoughts and emotions. Showing the emotion of happiness by smiling or the emotion of anger by yelling are the behaviors we all know well. All of us know people who have mastered specific competencies (skills) in life, but some inadequate or inappropriate behaviors have diluted their competencies, which in turn, compromises their ability to perform at high levels. So these people, although full of skill/talent, let their innate talent go to waste because of poor behavior. In golf, when things do go wrong, it is the responsive behavior that everyone sees.

Behavior is a response. Make no mistake about it. It is a response (not cause) to your brain's interpretation of an experience.

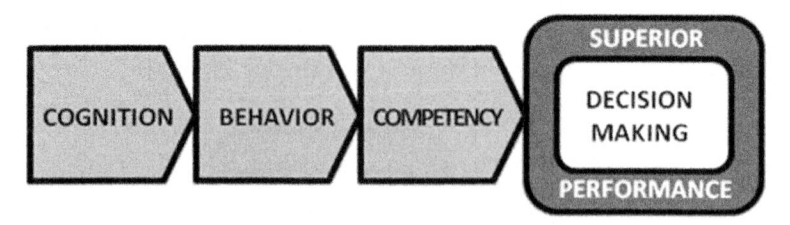

Figure 4. Cognition & Behavior

Cognition

Cognition precedes behavior. Slightly oversimplifying this concept, cognition refers to one's intellectual capacities, thoughts, knowledge, and memories. This is the rational part of our brain. In effect, it is our ability to take data points, weave them together in some cogent manner, and reach a conclusion that dictates (consciously or subconsciously) what behavior to exhibit. If your thinking leads to the wrong conclusion, the rest of the steps in the sequence to good decision-making get compromised no matter how competent (skilled) you are.

You can now begin to see all the pieces of decision-making in a sequence where each preceding dimension can trump the proceeding dimension.

"Every time you lose, you think that life's unfair. You think of the bad breaks. But when you're winning and playing well, you still get those bad breaks, only you overcome them. It just depends on how strong your mind is." -Greg Norman

Emotional Intelligence (EQ)

What finally precedes cognition in this physiological sequence to decision-making (high performance) is your Emotional Intelligence (EQ).

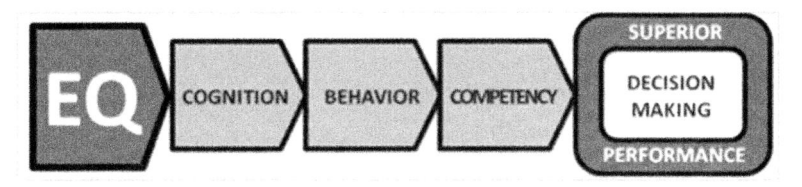

Figure 5. Emotional Intelligence (EQ)

What you see above is the neurological sequence in the brain of human beings for all decision-making, whether it is athletic or in day-to-day life. Emotions are the first neurological response by your body, the equipment. Your physical body is an equipment that you want to manipulate correctly for a required shot. **Everything in your body and brain is dictated first by your emotions**. Emotions lead to thinking, which leads to behavior, which is the uniform you wear as you perform your skills. You can see how easily it is for your skills to be compromised, especially in the heat of battle as they are so farther down the sequence. Skills stand no chance against the power of your emotions and how your brain is interpreting stimuli, especially in real time (game time) when everything seemingly is at stake, and happening at warp speed.

Our five senses aggressively and constantly send signals to the prefrontal lobes of the brain located in our forehead area. This is the 'port of entry' of all stimuli. Everything we see, hear, feel, touch, and smell gets sent here for primarily one purpose: to assign a threat rating to that experience. Happening in microseconds, the higher the threat level, the more the secretion of powerful hormones like cortisol (fear) which can cause high states of anxiety. The lower the threat level, the smoother the transition into the subsequent steps of the diagram above allowing you to think clearly, behave appropriately, and ultimately perform to your ability.

"Of all the hazards, fear is the worst." -Sam Snead

Neuroscience of "Pressure"

The terms anxiety, nerves, pressure, disoriented, stress, heat-of-battle, choking, being-in-the-zone, and the like, are used not only in all sports, but also everyday life. Let us dig deeper into understanding our body, the equipment, in the context of these terms.

Our brain is the only place where all our cognitive functions reside. Cognitive functions include our long-term, short-term, and working memory. Put simply, the brain is *both* our filing cabinet and command center to make decisions. For example, if you have just learned how to do a high flop shot, that learning sits in your brain, not in your hands or arms. There is no such thing as muscle memory. Muscles do not have any memory cells or neuropathic abilities. You can train your muscles and body parts new motor skills, but in terms of the command to execute those new skills, that comes from the brain. A person in a coma whose body is perfectly normal is unable to perform any physical activity because the command center, the brain, is disabled. **Everything you know and have learned is stored in the brain.** The same brain that you are using in golf is also where all of your life's experiences are stored. This is a key point in the context of underperforming as athletes often wonder post-round why they made poor decisions, or say "in hindsight" they may have made better decisions and hit different shots.

From the command center, the brain, all orders are sent to different parts of the body. The body itself cannot do anything without the brain. The brain sends all its instructions through the spinal cord. In other words, the spinal cord is like a bundle of cables for that critical information from memory banks to be sent to parts of your body. Now, as shown in the next image, conveniently located between the spinal cord and the brain—between the command center and cables—is the amygdala.

Low emotion
(calm, relaxed)

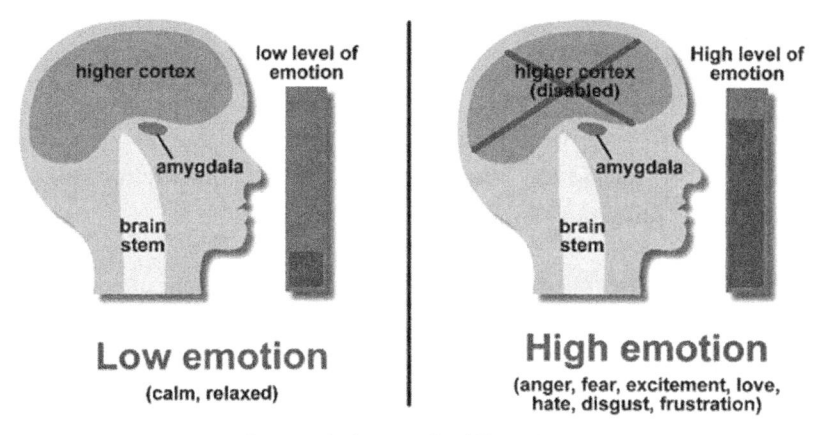

High emotion
(anger, fear, excitement, love, hate, disgust, frustration)

Figure 6. Impact of Emotions

The Instinctive Emotional Response

The amygdala is a gland that secretes hormones in your body, as described earlier. It is situated there because its job is to respond according to the directions of the prefrontal lobes – the threat center. The prefrontal lobes sit in your forehead area. Microseconds of sensing a potential threat, the amygdala (and other glands) releases hormones in your body that either partially or entirely disables your brain. This disabling of cognitive functions enables your body to respond quickly and instinctively to that danger. This is essentially a safety mechanism, which is triggered as a reaction to every threat, regardless of whether the danger is perceived or real. *Our bodies have spent thousands of years morphing into this state so that we can perform our primary function: recognize danger and react to survive.* This is no different than most other living organisms. Although there are some universal physical dangers, such as someone pointing a gun at you, most emotional threats have no standards. It is different for everyone and based entirely on our past experiences, our memory banks, and mostly from our childhood or previous failures.

For example, if you're crossing a road and you see a car coming at you from the corner of your eye, you would—without thinking—instinctively jump or run to get the heck out of the way. You would not think about it; you would not analyze, "I wonder how fast the car is going. What are my options here?" If you did that—if you used the cognitive functions of your brain—you would not be able to respond fast enough and you would be hit. So the brain has to be disabled quickly for you to instinctively jump out of the way of the car.

Similarly, because it is the same brain, cognitive functions are disabled when golfers get into situations that they perceive as danger, such as going to the first tee knowing all of a sudden you have gone from hitting inconsequential shots on the range to a very consequential shot. The physiological response in the body at the first tee is virtually identical to that of a car coming at us. In other words, the amygdala does not make the distinction between the threat of a car coming at us and the threat of the consequences of a bad first tee shot. They are both threats, one is physical and the other is emotional.

"Putts get real difficult the day they hand out the money." -Lee Trevino

Look at the body's physiological automatic and instinctive response to anything perceived as a negative experience, depicted in Figure 7. In this state, just look at the impact of negative emotions on the physical body, the same body that you need to hit a golf shot. No athlete can perform at their best in this state. **This is akin to being physically injured!** In every round, as already discussed, a golfer is guaranteed to be in this state. And even if something does not go wrong, body fatigue, peer pressure and life pressure, all force the amygdala to do its instinctive job.

This physiological state leads to a "high alert state" where the brain is operating in "lock down mode" similar to the scenario of the speeding car approaching. The following consequences apply in this state:

- Have decreased cognitive performance.
- Have less oxygen available for critical brain functions.
- Tend to over generalize.

- Respond with defensive action.
- Perceive small stressors as worse than they actually are.
- Are easily aggravated.
- Recollection of past negative experiences.
- Will struggle to get along with others.
- Cannot perform at your best.

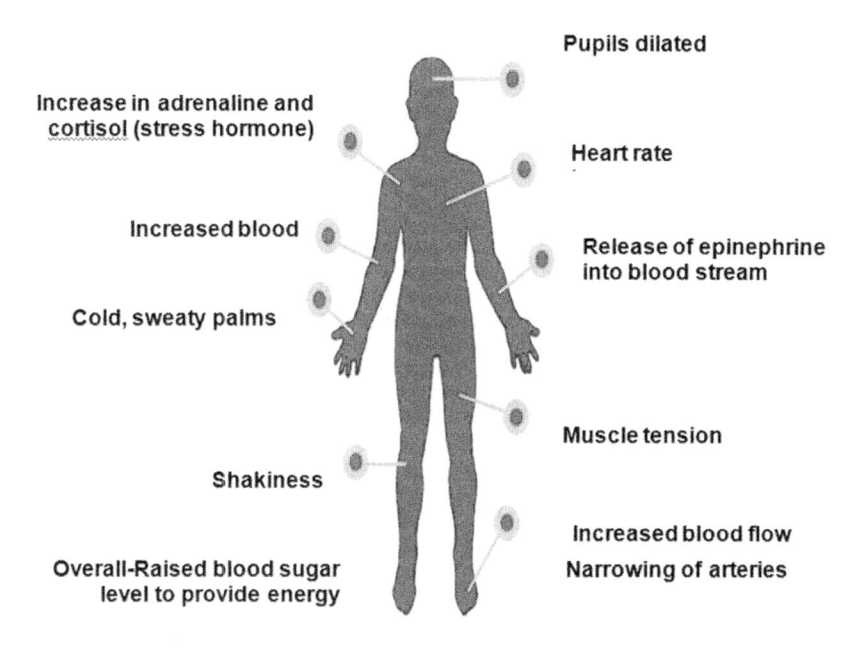

Pupils dilated

Increase in adrenaline and cortisol (stress hormone)

Heart rate

Increased blood

Release of epinephrine into blood stream

Cold, sweaty palms

Muscle tension

Shakiness

Increased blood flow
Narrowing of arteries

Overall-Raised blood sugar level to provide energy

Figure 7. The Body's Auto-Responsive Physiology

This state leads to those negative monologues – where we doubt our training, question our will, and recall past negative situations unintentionally. At that point, access to our rational ability and skill memory has been disabled and we are in the instinctive fight-or-flight mode. Again, no golfer can perform their best in this state. They simply are hijacked by their own bodies in the most natural and instinctive of ways. It is a virtual guarantee that every golfer will be in this state several times during a round. The question then becomes of how to manage this state, and this is where emotional intelligence (EQ) comes in.

"The object of golf is to beat someone. Make sure that someone is not yourself." -Bobby Jones

Negative Monologues

There is arguably no greater threat to an athlete than his or her own negative monologue. We all have them, not just in golf but in life as well. You know the ones where you talk to yourself about all the reasons why you cannot or should not do something, where you recall the worse memories, and seriously doubt your ability to perform. There is no athlete or human being who actively pursues a negative monologue. They happen without choice, and very often at the most inopportune of times.

Conversely, athletes often say that when they are at their best, in the proverbial zone, that there is no such negative monologue. In fact, the calm state is almost euphoric as though everything is exactly how it should be and you are performing magic.

In golf, an endurance sport of many hours, you are certain to have both types of dialogues. I will discuss at length how to manage your emotions and these dialogues; but it is important to understand how the negative ones, more harmful to your performance, are created.

Let us say you had 10 experiences yesterday and nine of them were spectacular ones – very positive - but one of them was negative. For example, the negative one may have been you accidentally touching a hot stove and slightly burning your hand while making coffee. Today, the day after, which experience do you think you will be remembering more? If you answered honestly, then it would be the negative one, not the nine other great positive ones. Why? Once again, our physiological design and construction from thousands of years takes center stage. Our brain has a specific place in the back of our skull where, in fact, negative memories are stored. When we have negative experiences in life, whether traumatic ones or like the slight hand burn, the brain needs to store them so that they can easily be retrieved. You NEED to remember the burned hand more than the nine positive experiences because the burned hand plays a larger role in your survival than your positive experiences. You need to remember to be careful next time you are near a hot stove.

In this manner, almost all of our life's negative experiences are not only permanently stored, but they are in fact the ones that are first retrieved if the prefrontal lobes (Threat Center) label a current experience as a negative one (one with potential threat). So as the amygdala disables the brain in high anxiety situations after getting word from the prefrontal lobes, your cognitive functions (making decisions, remembering how to do routine skills) are further limited to those negative memories and, thus, the negative monologues. A golfer who was nervous going to the first tee recalls that he remembered what another golfer had just said on the range about yet another player earlier who hit his first shot out of bounds. Even though it was not his own experience, given that his brain was on alert, he then recalled his own worst shot that he had not thought of in years. This is all happening because our brain is searching for context for the threat alert.

It is, therefore, very important for a golfer to take inventory of those past negative experiences so that he or she is, at a bare minimum, aware of what they are and can anticipate the nature of the negative monologues when they occur. In this book, you will learn how to do this as well as how to proactively induce positive monologues during the round but more importantly, during those unpredictable mishaps.

Exercise: Your Negative Memory Bank

Make a list of the experiences of your life that you feel are possibly stored in your negative memory bank

1. _____

2. _____

3. _____

4. _____

5. _____

Exercise: Your Negative Monologues

Make a list of most common negative monologues you typically have with yourself after a bad shot

1. _____

2. _____

3. _____

4. _____

5. _____

> ### *Exercise: Your Positive Monologues*
>
> **Make a list of the most common positive monologues you have with yourself (when you are in a zone)**
>
> 1. _____
>
> 2. _____
>
> 3. _____
>
> 4. _____
>
> 5. _____

"Success depends almost entirely on how effectively you manage the game's two ultimate adversaries: the course and yourself." -Jack Nicklaus

How to Increase your EQ

The first step in increasing your EQ is to learn to take your emotional temperature. Imagine an old thermometer – the kind you stick in your mouth. Imagine there are only three recordings it can give you – GREEN, YELLOW, and RED - similar to that of a traffic light.

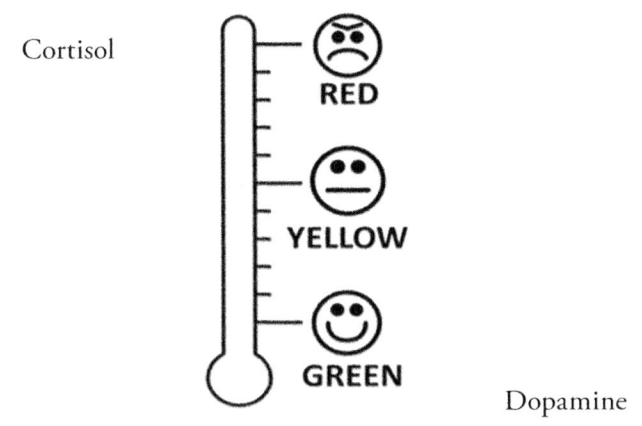

Figure 8. Emotional Thermometer

Green indicates that you are comfortable, happy, stress-free, can think clearly and perform well. Now that you understand the neuroscience behind GREEN, you will note that the prefrontal lobes have sent a low threat level signal to the amygdala while in this state. This essentially means your brain, where all of the memories of your training and strategy are stored, can easily retrieve skills, memories, and make good decisions—the center piece of your performing at your best. It also means that the negative memories do not have to be accessed, which enhances your chances of being in a zone, since only positive monologues occur here. GREEN is a good temperature reading. You can learn how to give yourself an accurate reading by referring to the diagram above showing the body's state when in the RED state. When GREEN, you will naturally feel relaxed, you will feel like all your senses are alert, you will naturally have positive monologues and recall positive experiences, you will remember all of your focal thoughts in all the parts of the game of golf, and you will feel like nothing can throw you off your game.

YELLOW temperature reading indicates that you are a little stressed and anxious. Something has gone wrong in the round, but it is not fatal. The wind picked up during your shot, or you hit a shot slightly left when you meant to hit it straight, or your ball landed in a divot – the list goes on and on of things that can go wrong and take us off "GREEN" to "YELLOW". You are not in green for sure because everything just described in GREEN is not happening, but you are also not in RED where the consequences are very serious. In YELLOW, negative dialogues are occurring, but you are able to recollect some positive ones too. It is an internal battle. Most of your round day may feel like this.

RED is when you are implicitly or explicitly out of control, filled with anger and rage, or disappointment and frustration. You are filled with negative monologues, even being abusive to yourself and perhaps others around you like your caddie or volunteers. You are looking to blame someone, instead of finding a solution. You are frustrated that you cannot think clearly or remember much. This happens when the perceived threat is interpreted in your brain as fatal – at this point, you feel missing your goal is imminent and very likely.

"When you're playing poorly, you start thinking too much. That's when you confuse yourself." –Greg Norman

This is a new language you are now learning to use in golf – green, yellow, and red. Identifying how your body is at any given point of the round. You can see now why it is so important to know your EQ temperature during the round. The good news is that taking your emotional temperature is not something you can only practice in a round or during practice. Remember how all decisions are made – not just golf ones? Everything starts with emotions, in and out of golf. So, no matter where you are or what you are doing, every three hours of a normal day starting today, take your emotional temperature and give yourself a color reading. Are you GREEN, YELLOW or RED? After about a week of this, start to do it more often, perhaps every hour and then start to do it during practice and the round. I recommend taking your EQ temperature before every shot during your round.

As stated earlier, ***the most difficult shot in golf is the one right after a bad one***. You know why now. After a bad shot, you are assured, without any active provocation from you, to retrieve other negative memories, disable your brain, and compromise your decision-making ability. You are either yellow or red after a bad shot. For this reason, this shot is the most difficult one because you are in an internal war now between your will and your instinctive biological state. Your body, your equipment has changed. Getting your body out of yellow or red and back to green is EQ. How to win this before you get to the next shot will be described in detail later.

You must become a master at taking your own temperature. You do not have a coach or team member out there during the round (unless you have a caddie who is a psychologist) who can help you do this. Clearly, if you are GREEN, then nothing needs to be done mentally or emotionally. Just keep going and maintain your focus. But if you are YELLOW or RED, in that 93% of time, then something has to happen to get you back to GREEN as fast as possible. If Jack Nicklaus said he only hit one shot a round that was perfect, then at least 60 other shots are going to put you, whether you are cognitively aware of it or not, in yellow or red. Research has shown that it is rare to go from GREEN directly to RED unless something very dramatic happens. Usually, we progress slowly into YELLOW without being aware of it, and stay in YELLOW for a while, at which point, nothing dramatic is required to elevate to RED since you are essentially a fuse just waiting to be lit. This is another common mistake many professional golfers make. They do not do enough when in YELLOW to get back to GREEN and often think they are mentally strong to go from RED directly back to GREEN. This can be done, but it is much harder.

Once you have learned how to take your EQ temperature, then and only then can you know how to regulate yourself back to GREEN.

The things you would do to go from YELLOW back to GREEN are very different from the things you would do to go from RED back to GREEN. Not every mishap is a RED. Missing a 40-foot putt is very different from missing a one-foot putt – emotionally.

To state the obvious, the goal is to stay in GREEN as much as possible. Note that this is an emotional state. Chapters 4 through 8 will discuss very specific mishap situations – emotional and mental- to help with typical scenarios in these legs of golf: in practice, pre-round, round, and post-round. In this chapter, by establishing these GREEN, YELLOW, and RED standards, you now have a language you can use with your friends and coaches to help you prepare in a customized manner.

Changing your Emotional Temperature: GREEN TO GREEN

Our five senses are the only connection our body, the equipment, has with ever-changing stimuli during golf. Before every shot, as you take your EQ temperature during a round, and you are GREEN, then the goal is to stay GREEN proactively. When already in GREEN, the best way to stay in GREEN is to actively overuse your five senses. This is called macro and micro FOCUS, and will be discussed in further detail in Chapter 4.

You would be using your eyes, for example, to focus on the smallest detail of whatever is in front of you. It might be dimples on the ball, or a blade of grass as a target, or the trees on the course, or specific colors on flowers. For FEEL, you would not just be feeling for the wind, but the air around you at every hole and even the air coming in and out of your lungs. Or even feel the energy transfer from your arms to the club and ball, or the sense of your hands on gripping your club or the ground as you walk. For SOUND, it would not be just listening for cheers from volunteers or playing partners, but also to the wind or birds or other sounds you normally would ignore. For TASTE, it can be allowing a sip of water or drink to sit in your mouth for a few seconds longer than normal or doing the same thing with any food.

Actively engaging the senses is a powerful technique to stay in the proverbial present, and to keep your self-awareness at a high state of alert. Think about it – if you are this focused and you notice that suddenly, for whatever reason you are not, then you know your emotional temperature has changed. Something has caused you to lose focus. It is hard to know you have lost focus if you never had it in the first place. I discuss focus in greater detail and how to use it in both training and rounds in Chapter 4. For now, learn to appreciate your five senses as a critical tool set in the equipment of your body.

"For me, winning isn't something that happens suddenly on the field when the whistle blows and the crowds roar. Winning is something that builds physically and mentally every day that you train and every night that you dream." -Emmitt Smith

Changing your Emotional Temperature: YELLOW TO GREEN

The absolute first thing to do when you take your EQ temperature and you are in YELLOW is to breathe. This might surprise you since you are probably thinking that you are always breathing – what is up with that? No. Change your breathing. Take a count (cadence) of how long it takes you to breathe in, and take another count of how long it takes you to breathe out in the same normal breath. For most people this normal breathing count is anywhere from 2-5 counts breathing in, and 2-5 counts breathing out. Practice right now and increase your breath count in to average about 25 and your breath count out to average about 25 also. You can do this by simply taking in your breath slower and releasing your breath longer in a very controlled manner. When the body physiologically is in YELLOW, recall that one of the symptoms is increased heart rate and increased breath rate. A lot of oxygen is being channeled to other parts of your body in anticipation of having to 'jump to avoid the car', but it is your brain that needs the oxygen. Slowing your breath by actively counting 25 in and 25 out, will slow down your heart rate, even if just a little at first and begin to disable the amygdala and enable the brain. You will recall it is only in your brain that all your skills reside. You need your memories of skills and what-to-do list. This kind of EQ breathing allows you to use some rational thought by putting the situation that caused you to go to YELLOW into context.

ACT (Abdomen, Chest, Throat) Breathing Technique

During physical activity, and especially during a round, there are essentially three levels of breathing that occur. The first is breathing at the throat (T) level – air tends not to feel like it goes anywhere deeper than your mouth. This is typically short and fast breaths where the breath-count in and out is less than 2. The second is chest (C) level, where the breaths are inhaled chest-deep with breath-counts in and out between 2 and 10. The last is abdomen (A) level, where a long slow breath in to the level your lungs feel like they are touching your abdomen, is followed by a long slow breath out.

During a round, most golfers are not thinking of their breath at all and allow it to be at the mercy of whatever happens. High anxiety situations also automatically trigger your body to the T level of breathing. This is instinctive and in response to the higher heart rate - which itself is a response by the body to prepare you for survival. Unlike cognitive or brain activity, breathing involves a lot of body parts and muscles and, therefore, can be controlled even after the initial burst of anxiety to T level breathing. This is the reason why it should always be the first step in managing EQ - because it is one of the easiest things to do. Though A level (abdomen) breathing is quite challenging to maintain during a round, your goal should be to always be breathing at A level during a round, especially in times of challenging conditions (wind, rain, etc.). I also recommend attempting A level breathing when you are GREEN. As you are training or playing, keep track of what level of ACT (Abdomen, Chest, Throat) you are doing and know you can perform best at the A level, so adjust your breathing accordingly. Learning this is key to building EQ strength.

The next step in changing your temperature from Yellow to Green is to create a YELLOW CARD. This card will change over time, and may be even several times, over the course of a season. Let's create your personalized yellow card first and then I will elaborate on how to use it to change the temperature (after breathing) from YELLOW to GREEN. Answer the five questions below with just three words or less that will instantly take you back emotionally to a very specific point in time and place.

Exercise: Your Yellow Card

1. When/where was the best round you have ever had?

---

2. List all your 14 clubs here and describe where you hit the best shot ever with each shot?

Driver _____
3 wood _____
_____

3 iron _____
4 iron _____
5 iron _____
6 iron _____
7 iron _____
8 iron _____
9 iron _____
PW _____
Wedge 1 _____
Wedge 2 _____
Putter _____

3. When/where was the best recovery shot you have hit?

> 4. When/where was the best first tee shot?
>
> 5. When/where was the best warm up to a round?

Transfer these questions and your responses to a yellow index card (for your pocket when playing) or perhaps onto your iPhone (during training) so that it is portable and can be with you when you need it.

Just as negative and threatening experiences have dire consequences to the chemistry of our body as explained earlier, positive experiences have the opposite effect. They can give us confidence by releasing dopamine, the counter hormone to cortisol (fear hormone) and inspire us to perform better. Research shows that it takes an average of five positive experiences to dilute a comparable negative experience. In other words, cortisol is more powerful than dopamine. Recall the burnt hand example from earlier versus the nine great things on that day. The problem during training, and especially during a round, is that we cannot predict when those positive experiences will happen, any more than we can predict when the negatives one will occur. However, we can be certain that it is very unlikely that the positive experiences will conveniently occur immediately as the negative one is happening so that they can counteract each other out. This is where the YELLOW card comes in. These five positive experiences can be induced into your physiological system to redirect the neuropathways. They are impossible to remember during the 'heat' of a round as you have so many competing thoughts and priorities, and therefore writing them down before hand is necessary. You will need this list to counteract the cause of what got you into YELLOW so you can get back to GREEN.

After your breathing, when in YELLOW, take a look at the YELLOW card you have crafted for yourself. It is critical that you have written down on a card for reading later when needed, as opposed to relying on memory. Forget how it will look like to a competitor – at this point, your biggest competitor is not another person, it is you.

When playing, as you read it, take just a minute to transport yourself emotionally to that great memory and remember what worked so well and what you are capable of doing. The breathing and the YELLOW card (induced positive counteracting experiences) will impact your prefrontal lobes, the grip of the amygdala, and allow you to do what you need to do to get back to focusing and to GREEN.

Take note that you are using both your emotions (by taking your temperature) and your thoughts first, prior to using your golf skills to get to performing at your best again – just as the sequential physiological decision-making model dictates.

If you look closely during rounds, you will often see a small photo of someone taped on a golfer's bag or yardage book. Maybe it is a picture of a loved one that has passed away, but looking at it provides inspiration that could carry him/her from YELLOW to GREEN. These pictures or mementos work in the same way, and often times bring an individual's emotions back from YELLOW to GREEN.

Hostage negotiators use this same technique when working with criminals who have taken hostages. They know the situation is red, the criminal is red, and so are the hostages. Their first goal is to emotionally 'diffuse' the situation to allow rational thought to have a chance. Sometimes, they will bring in the wife or child of the criminal to talk to them directly. Hearing their voices can be a very powerful dilutor of red emotions that can allow for a safe resolution.

When in yellow or red, you are your own hostage negotiator as you are being held captive emotionally and cognitively by thousands of years of design and your own negative memories.

Changing your Emotional Temperature: RED TO GREEN

When something terrible has occurred and you have taken your emotional temperature and diagnosed yourself as RED, the first step is again to immediately breathe in the same way as the process for YELLOW to GREEN. This will be a little harder, but more important, to do. Try your best to get to A Level (Abdomen) of breathing. In RED, your breathing will be very intense (T level), your heart rate very high and your vision blurred, just to a mention a few symptoms.

The process to go from RED to GREEN is similar to the YELLOW transformation. You need to create a RED card, but the content will be very different. You will still need to induce positive experiences, but they have to be of a very different and very powerful kind.

> My first Ironman race as a pro was in 2002 at Ironman Wisconsin. One reason I became a professional was because I wanted to do the Wisconsin race as that was near my hometown of Sussex. I spent the year training, going to Madison and working on the course, and was very confident going into it. I attended the press conference, which I was not invited to, but still went and listened. No one knew who I was. Listening to the pro women, I still had belief in myself and that I could win. I registered and received my lucky number 33 and thought I was all ready. During the race I had a fabulous win. I saw the top pro ahead of me and passed her on the bike with all media camera on me now! I had a phenomenal bike ride, but when I got off the bike my legs hurt so badly that I couldn't run. I ran anyway but couldn't keep up, started walking and got passed. Half way, on the sidelines I saw my daughter and mother-in-law, both in their wheelchairs, screaming for me, and thought how awful that I was feeling sorry for myself for having aching legs. They would have given anything to walk just a mile. I ran over- gave them a hug and high five, and started running again with only their faces on my mind, and won the Ironman.
>
> -Heather Gollnick
>
> 5-Time Ironman Champion

Though Heather's story above has nothing to do with golf, it is very powerful and clearly was incredibly effective to get her from almost not finishing at the half way mark of the run, to winning the Ironman in 2002; and underscores just how powerful emotions can be. The same applies to golf. You, however, may not have your daughter and mother-in-law in a wheelchair in your round, and do not need to, to orchestrate a similar transformation in yourself during a RED state situation. You can self-induce similarly powerful experiences by completing the RED card below. The RED card, unlike the YELLOW one, rarely changes and is used in those rare RED situations we all hope not to have.

Your personalized RED Card: Answer the five questions below with just three words or less that will instantly take you back to that point in memory, time and place.

Exercise: Your Red Card

1. What are the first names of the most important people in your life?

---

2. What are the first names of your best friends – the ones that will be your friends for life?

---

3. When/where was the place you have been happiest in your life?

---

4. Who is the person, dead or alive, that you aspire to be like off the golf course and why?

---

5. What are you most proud of in your life – an accomplishment not given to you that no one can ever take from you?

The yellow and red experiences are YOUR positive experiences and one of the more under-utilized assets you have. You know your brain will neurologically attract YOUR negative memories when in yellow or red. It is designed to do so. Your job is to attract positive ones at the right time, after a bad shot, between shots, so that you can make the best decision for the next shot and allow your physical body to do what you have trained it to do and know you are capable of doing.

Now, let's redefine Emotional strength:

Emotional strength is the amount of time it takes to convert a negative thought to a positive one.

Emotional strength is the amount of time it takes to go from yellow to green.

Emotional strength is the amount of time it takes to go from red to green.

Top 3 Ideas *I learned from this chapter*
1.
2.
3.
3 Action Steps *I will take immediately to incorporate the above learning into my practice and competitive rounds*
1.
2.
3.

Chapter Summary

1. Your goal needs to be to perform at your best during the round that matters. This means making good decisions.
2. The physiological sequence of making good decisions starts with our emotions, not our skills or thinking. Therefore, understanding emotions is critical to optimal performance.
3. All our golf skills are stored in our brain, and in no other part of our body. The brain can be shut off as an instinctive survival response to any danger, perceived or real. When the brain is disabled, then poor decisions are made.
4. Knowing your emotional temperature at all times of the round is critical to your performance. There are 3 EQ Temperature readings: GREEN, YELLOW, and RED.
5. The goal is to stay GREEN as much as possible during a round by using the ACT Breathing Model and your five senses to focus.
6. If in YELLOW or RED, use cards (or similar approach) to induce positive experiences (dopamine) to counteract the impact of any mishap (cortisol).
7. These techniques begin to lay the foundation of being a golfer with high EQ.

Chapter 3

I am fortunate enough to have a profession where having authentic conversations is part of my job. I hear many stories from very accomplished people. What they have in common is well researched and documented already, and of the many shared attributes of these folks, I enjoy listening to that 'one experience' they all have - after which - their self-confidence is impenetrable. It may waiver from time to time with failure and success, but the belief that they are special enough to do great things is forever imprinted in their DNA.

What these stories have in common is what I call "the one experience." It may have been a fear of speaking in front of a large audience. They can tell me of the time when "it" happened – everything went well and they were never afraid of it again. Athletically, it may be the first marathon which was previously an inconceivable proposition and then after, they cannot wait to do more, and do them faster. If you paused right now at this point of the blog and took inventory of your life experiences, I bet you could think of one yourself.

Now, as positive as all this sounds, what should be troubling is that we do not have enough of these and in fact, do not actively pursue them, and they pile up on the proverbial regret list. Yet, if you think again of your "one experience" in whatever endeavor it occurred, you would be hard-pressed to find logical reasons why that cannot happen in other areas of your life. This week, begin the process of orchestrating a new "one experience." Find a YouTube video, an article, a person, anything … of someone already doing what you want to be able to do. Study it. Get a coach. Practice it. Copy it.

Stumble and fall. Use these interim failures as stepping stones to that "one experience" you know will happen.

https://izzyjustice.wordpress.com/2014/08/04/that-one-experience/

Art and Science of Learning

Golf requires a good bit of IQ (intellectual intelligence) as cognitive functions are put to the test. This was discussed earlier, but it is worth now making the distinction more clear.

There are essentially three categories of skills that are tested in the game of golf:

1. Golf Skills
2. Mental Skills
3. Emotional Skills

Golf skills are obvious: your swing, ability to hit all kinds of shots in the long and short game, and putting. As stated earlier, this book does not cover any of these and so many other golf-specific physical skills that most golfers spend the majority of their time practicing.

Mental skills are cognitive (IQ) related. These are the data points of every shot that are used to make decisions on what type of shot to hit. While reading a putt, for example, your cognitive functions realize that it is uphill with no break. Your brain then makes a decision to hit it firm and straight. Once the decision is made, then the golf skill of a putting stroke is used to execute that decision. Mental strength is having the experience to know the best decision to make. Mental strength is not emotional strength. You may have the ability to process the above putt in the manner described and the physical ability to hit the putt purely (golf skill), but if just before you hit that putt, you recall the last putt you just hit in a similar situation which you missed, and you lose focus, then the emotional trauma of the previous putt will trump both your mental strength and your golf skill as discussed earlier in the decision-making sequence.

Course management is also a part of mental strength, and not emotional strength. Knowing what club to hit off the tee box to give you the best approach shot on each hole is part of course management. Having a pre-determined strategy for every hole, and a plan B in the event conditions like wind impact that strategy, is also part of mental strength. These kinds of mental strength, proper decision-making, have been discussed in many books and videos and not the purpose of this book. This is an area of much improvement for most golfers, but I argue that it is not a lack of mental strength that ultimately leads to under-performance as most decisions of this nature are relatively easy to learn and process. What leads to compromising this decision-making is the EQ part that every golfer has to negotiate through.

Moving forward, this book will be specific in drawing attention to these three areas of skills so as to properly delineate and learn from.

Golf encompasses not just the obvious disciplines of long game and short game, but several others in order to perform well during a round. These include strength and flexibility, nutrition, recovery, game-day strategy, and equipment. Based on the course, you and/or your coach will create a plan that calibrates all this to your ability and goals. The point here is that unlike single discipline sports, there is a lot more to learn, to master, and to manage. Being very good at learning itself is, therefore, another skill that Athletes often over-look yet, it is very necessary to optimize both practice on the range as well as during a round.

Let's take two golfers, Jill and Pam, of equal handicap, coached by the same coach, and who both had a four-hour practice on the range yesterday. Both of them reported to their coaches, tweeted and posted on Facebook to their golf club friends that they completed their lengthy practice. When the coach debriefed with both Jill and Pam, she learned that these identical practice sessions were executed very differently. Pam was very focused, did each drill specifically as directed and hit exactly the shots required after each drill. Pam shared several observations based on this data with her coach to discuss potential changes. The *purpose* of the workout was met. Jill, however, was distracted. She had a personal situation with her boyfriend that was not going well and her mind kept wandering towards solutions for the relationship. While she completed all of her practice, her focus was on and off, and as a result, she was inconsistent in her performance. Some of the shots were good and others were not. Some drills were done and others were not. As expected, her follow up session with her coach was not very productive. It was hard for her coach to know whether any of the issues Jill had were related to golf or her lack of focus. Jill's practice, though commendable for the four-hours put in, was not nearly as good of a learning experience as that of Pam. Although both golfers put in four hours of practice, clearly the value to each was totally different.

This chapter is included in the book because EQ comes into play in your ability to learn as well, not just to perform during a round. Golf is a unique game in that there are dozens of golf and mental skills required. Hitting a driver at 100 mph is quite different from hitting a three-foot putt, yet both are often done in one hole. There are dozens of types of shots even with a single club that can be executed. There is a lot to learn in this multidiscipline sport of golf.

"Golf is evolving, every day, every shot." -Tiger Woods

In this chapter, I will explore the art and science of learning. The objective is to have you become very comfortable with making mistakes, especially during practice, and then to be able to have a framework to process those mistakes into learning that can stick with you for future practice and rounds. Learning from mistakes is an emotional exercise as much as it is a technical exercise. I have addressed the EQ component of being a golfer, but wanted to focus on the technical components of good learning in this chapter. Golf, after all, is a game of mishaps. The skill is not to avoid them, but to learn from them when they occur.

Learning can occur proactively, as demonstrated by Pam in the example above, where mistakes are induced. This can be done using a trial and error approach to figure out what works and what does not. Learning can also be reactive where the mishap occurs as a by-product of the practice or round, often unplanned, but equally valuable for learning. As there is so much to learn in golf, it is critical that to be good at golf, you must inherently be good at learning.

Myth about Learning

There is a misperception about learning that has spread quite rapidly. It is from Malcolm Gladwell's 10,000 Rule from his book *Outliers: The Story of Success*, which, incidentally, is a great read. Many coaches in all sports are convincing athletes that based on the research of the book, in which Gladwell has suggested that it takes 10,000 hours to fully learn a skill and become an expert at it, that volume (repetition) exclusively is the key to mastery. This has resulted in very high repetitive and volume-based training in many sports, often at the expense of focused and learning-based training. In the example of the range practice for Jill and Pam, clearly those four hours were not equal. Similarly, it could be argued that it may take Jill several four-hour sessions to accomplish what Pam did in her one session.

What Gladwell actually said was that it takes 10,000 hours to be a phenom, of which there are literally only a handful in the world; men and women who consistently perform at extra-ordinary levels and are often known by one name like Jordan, Elway, Mozart, Chrissie, Phelps, and Tiger. In golf, this applies to the less than 1% golfers within the professional ranks.

While I fully appreciate the need for range time, the point worth reiterating here is that you must make a distinction in your practice between 'logging in the hours' and 'training with a learning purpose.'

I will show you how to do the latter in this chapter, which will allow you to be a much smarter learner and golfer, optimizing the limited time you have as a working professional.

"I never hit a shot, even in practice, without having a very sharp, in-focus picture of it in my head." -Jack Nicklaus

Traditional Learning

Most of us have formally learned in the same general methodology. It was the methodology used in most schools at all levels across the world. In the broadest sense, the methodology is based on academic models of memory and testing. Information was given to you in a classroom or other setting, and then you demonstrated that you acquired that knowledge at that specific time period (for example, a semester) by being tested on examinations by answering questions. I concede I am over simplifying academia, but only to underscore the point that I believe learning has historically been very flawed.

As an adult, you learn best at the *point of need*. This means that if you are going to build a cabinet in your house this upcoming weekend, then the best time in your life to learn about building cabinets are the next few days just before the weekend. Could you have learned a few weeks ago? Yes. Could you learn a few weeks from today? Yes. But now is the best time to learn because you have a need this weekend that necessitates knowledge. Your emotions and appetite to learn are at a peak. In the traditional learning model that most of us have been taught, the need is a false need – it's an examination at a specified time in the academic pipeline – not a true application of what you have learned in the semester. Some estimate that people forget almost all the courses they took in college within five years of graduating, often because what they have learned in the five years after graduating was much more experiential and relevantly applicable to needs (job). For golfers, the opportunity to learn in every practice is not just a philosophical argument, but very much a real one.

Another reason I believe why traditional learning models are flawed is that they typically have been designed to fit only one style of personality and learning. Extensive research in adult learning over the past 20 years has revealed that there are, in fact, many styles of learning, with no one being 'better' than the other. The key is to find out what type of learner you are and then seek to do your practice and learning in that modality. Given this, it is important for golfers to find coaches that are flexible enough to match their style.

Some good questions worth asking yourself are: how good of a learner are you? What methodology do you follow to learn? How often does learn translate to desired outcomes?

Learning Styles

According to Neil Fleming's VARK Model, there are several learning styles. It is important to know your style. Note that your style may vary based on the specific need you have, the urgency of that need, and the availability of resources to learn. The styles are:

- Visual (spatial): You prefer using pictures, images, and spatial understanding.
- Aural (auditory-musical): You prefer using sound and music.
- Verbal (linguistic): You prefer using words, both in speech and writing.
- Physical (kinesthetic): You prefer using your body, hands and sense of touch.
- Logical (mathematical): You prefer using logic, reasoning and systems.
- Social (interpersonal): You prefer to learn in groups or with other people.
- Solitary (intrapersonal): You prefer to work alone and use self-study.

What is your style and how can you modify how you learn to match this style? This could be either on your own or with a coach.

Learning Agility

What is actually more important than knowing your learning style is to have the desire to want to learn all the time. This is called having *learning agility*. Golfers who perform optimally have very high learning agility. In general, people who have high learning agility live healthier and more successful lives. They view almost all experiences as an opportunity to learn and in fact, embrace weaknesses or mistakes as *the* reason to work harder and more effectively.

Not just in the examples above, but also in all other sports, I have seen incredible transformation in athletes who previously thought they were the hardest working athletes in their sport only to realize that they had not been learning nearly as effectively as they could have been. So make a commitment to learn from every practice and round, and apply it in your next experience. Let me show you how.

"I've missed more than 9000 shots in my career. I've lost almost 300 games. 26 times, I've been trusted to take the game winning shot and missed. I've failed over and over and over again in my life. And that is why I succeed." -Michael Jordan

Learning Methodology

There is both an art and a science to learning. In the methodology I recommend, there is a blend between the art and science as well as a key third dimension designed to make sure that once you have learned something, there is a process to then make it stick. I call this last step the 7-7 Rule.

Given that so much of learning in golf is trial and error, when something "clicks" it is even more important to find ways to make that something last for as long as possible.

The Art of Learning

The art is the emotional component that I have already discussed in Chapter 2. In both proactive and reactive learning, it is important to be in GREEN in order to learn. If you are YELLOW (as was likely the case with Jill) or RED (as was the case with the examples in Chapter 1), then your learning is compromised before your practice even begins. The first step for Jill could have been to take her emotional temperature on her way to the range and upon realizing she was YELLOW, to then read her YELLOW card to allow her to get back to GREEN before ever hitting a ball. In addition, Jill may be well served to also have YELLOW CARD-LIKE focal memories during her practice with brief and intermittent breaks to review her YELLOW CARD. This is much better than just going through the motions of hitting shots that Jill ended up doing.

"You're going to make mistakes. The key is to learn from them as fast as possible and make changes as soon as you can. That's not always easy to do because ego and pride get in the way." -Tiger Woods

The Science of Learning

Once in GREEN, then the science of learning comes into play for both proactive learning (planned experiences) and reactive learning (unplanned experiences).

Below is a very simple 5-Step general template that I encourage you to use dozens of times, or for at least six months. This template has instructions for completion. There is a 'clean version' of the template at the end of this chapter for you to complete and a completed template example provided as well.

Exercise: Learning Template Instructions

1. **Problem Statement:** Each learning can only have ONE problem. You cannot have two or more problems in one template. A common barrier to learning is the tangled-up nature of how we think about a problem. In addition, the problem statement is brief and NO SOLUTION OR CAUSE can be part of this statement.
2. **Symptoms of Problem:** There should not be more than 3 symptoms and if there are actually more, then pick the top 3. In addition, each symptom should be described in less than 5 words.
3. **Potential Root Causes:** Each root cause must be directly related to the symptom. If it is not, then it is not a root cause. There should not be more than 3 potential root causes and if there are actually more, then pick the top 3. In addition, each root cause should be described in less than 5 words.
4. **Sources for Solution:** There should not be more than 3 sources and if there are actually more, then pick the top 3. In addition, each source should be described in less than 5 words.
5. **Potential Solutions:** Each solution must directly address the root cause in step 3.The only way to know this is to try the solution and see if an impact is made to the symptoms in Step 2. There should not be more than 3 solutions and if there are more, then pick the top 3. In addition, each solution should be described in less than 5 words. These solutions could be from one or more of the sources in Step 4.

Exercise: Learning Template

1. Problem Statement: _____

2. Symptoms of Problem:
   a. _____

   b. _____

   c. _____

3. Potential Root Causes:
   a. _____

   b. _____

   c. _____

4. Sources for Solution:
   a. _____

   b. _____

   c. _____

5. Potential Solutions:
   a. _____

   b. _____

   c. _____

Sample Completed Learning Template (Pam)

1. Problem Statement: I always struggle the first few holes in a round and then I seem to settle down after the 3rd or 4th hole.

2. Symptoms of Problem:
  a. Higher scores in the first 3-4 holes

  b. I felt uncomfortable emotionally

  c. n/a

3. Potential Root Causes:
  a. I was nervous

  b. I felt I was too quick in my swing

  c. My putting was also too quick

4. Sources for Solution:
  a. My coach

  b. Have Jill watch me for my body position

  c. Watch a You Tube video

5. Potential Solutions: (after talking to coach & Jill)
  a. Focus on tempo in warm up

  b. Focus on finishing backswing

  c. Breath to abdomen 20-20 and get yourself to green before every shot

Of all athletes, professional golfers have some of the best opportunities to be learners. They have a good bit of time between shots, and after they have hit a bad one, they have time to think about it and even discuss it with their caddies before the next shot. But more importantly, what they do particularly well, and you can see this on TV most weekends, is that they recognize that the *best* time to learn is right after a bad shot. This is also true for amateurs and all athletes. In the earlier example, the best time for Pam to learn is within 24 hours of her session. After this, research shows that the emotional state (art) has altered significantly and you have moved on to other parts of your training or life in general. With so much stimuli, Pam's best appetite to learn, i.e., her learning agility, is at its peak immediately after her bad shots as she wrestles with why some of her shots are poor. In this example, the first four steps could be done immediately. This is what makes a good learner. Our general tendency is to skip the first four steps and immediately get to the solutions. A hasty approach often results in poor learning, creation of additional issues, and most notably, reinforcement of all bad habits (remember what the brain does with bad memories from Chapter 2).

"Winning is not always the barometer of getting better." -Tiger Woods

There is a reason almost all professional golfers have a swing coach. There is recognition of the dozens of moving parts in a golf swing and dozens of shots required that all of them have to come together for a good round. Another set of eyes from a trained coach is primarily a training aid for the golfers to do exactly what I am talking about above – to see what is wrong, figure out what is causing it, explore options and get it corrected. The average golfer does not have the luxury of a full time coach, but can certainly make herself a better learner.

I recommend, as almost all professional golfers and coaches can attest to, to make your practice very focused and use the templates above to make learning an integral part of your practice.

The 7-7 Rule

The 7-7 Rule states that in order to instill new learning, it has to be experienced in 7 different ways at 7 different times within 7 days. The 7-7 Rule is designed to help you make sure that new learning has the optimal stickiness factor, so that it can be imprinted and retrieved by your brain when it is needed the most. It is designed to prevent you from going to play a round after several good practice sessions on the range only to forget what you learned. Done correctly, it can significantly cut down those 10, 000 hours of mastery required. Repetition is an archaic way of imprinting new skills. In the world we live in today, the sheer volume of experiences vying for mind-share is enormous. A golfer has to give performance learning an added and proactive nudge to make sure it gets imprinted. *Note that one of the 7 ways has to be a negative imprint.* That is, it has to be the incorrect way of doing things, or simply put, your old way of doing things. The 7-7 Rule is based on three concepts that are being weaved together for the first time in this book.

1. Structure and Accountability

The first of the three is research done by Dr. Gail Matthews on accomplishing goals. Take a look at the table below.

Table 1. Achieving Goal Success

	Group 1	Group 2-3	Group 4	Group 5
Think about goals	✓	✓	✓	✓
Write about goals	✗	✓	✓	✓
Share with a friend	✗	✗	✓	✓
Weekly **progress report** to friend	✗	✗	✗	✓
Success Rate	43%	56%	64%	76%

Her study demonstrates powerfully the value of having structure and peer support in accomplishing desired goals. The more of both, the better the chances of achieving goals. The same applies to making something new stick.

2. Kinesiology

The second concept is based on the neuroscience of kinesiology, the study of human kinetics combined with memory formation, specifically of new neuropathways (ways of thinking). It essentially suggests that while learning, and in order to create stronger imprints (new neuropathways) in our brain, then all five senses (hear, feel, sight, smell, taste) must be collectively involved in the learning. In other words, the more engaged and experiential your learning, the greater the probability of it sticking.

3. 3-1 EQ Visualization Ratio

The third concept is based on the 3-1 EQ Visualization Ratio. This suggests that 3 EQ-based repetitions (non-physical) are equivalent to one physical repetition of an exercise. For example, if you are laying in bed, and you combine powerful visualization with imagination to recall a new learning three times, it is as good to your brain as actually doing the exercise physically once. In fact, researchers at the Cleveland Clinic Foundation demonstrated that mental training alone can sometimes induce muscle strength and new patterns.

It is often implied when using the term visualization that you are referring to the future. You are often told to visualize success, or a goal, or a desired outcome before it has happened. There are so many good quotes out there from inspiring people on the power of dreaming about something better in the future. This is all good. It is healthy to lay in bed dreaming about something you have not done, something you want to achieve, or something no one has thought of. The emotional power from these kinds of exercises is tremendous, often resulting in confidence, courage, and hope, which are priceless emotions to have during training and game day.

Because the past is filled with both positive and negative experiences, unlike the future where neither has occurred, we tend to not visualize or dream about the past. It seems counter intuitive at first pass. Why waste time visualizing something you have already done? *Well, I argue that visualizing something successful that you have already done is actually more empowering than visualizing something in the future where you have not done it yet. It is easier to visualize the past simply because you were there, you have all the details of the training day when you had an "aha" moment or events where you performed at your best.* You know where you were, how it happened, who else was there, and how it felt like emotionally. The past seems to get a bad rap as a place where only bad experiences exist and as such, we forget what a great place it can be to give us confidence, courage, and hope – as described in crafting the yellow and red cards. Instead of standing on the tee box visualizing a shot you want to hit but have not, why not visualize a similar shot you have actually hit from your yellow card? The 3:1 EQ Ratio is, therefore, a powerful tool that golfers should learn as an integral part of training. During a round, however, it is hard to visualize anything as so much is going on. This is why the information on your GREEN, YELLOW and RED cards is all about data points from the past since they are so much easier to recall, than trying to visualize something in the future. **I recommend that in lieu if visualizing the shot you want to hit, which has not happened yet, visualize a similar shot you have already hit and simply trust that you can duplicate.**

Let's go back to the session on the range that Jill and Pam had and apply all three concepts to see how we can make learning stick. As a result of being a proactive learner and demonstrating high learning agility, Pam went back to the range with Jill and almost immediately was told by Jill that her back swing got shorter which caused her to come down faster. This made sense as Pam said she felt quick.

Although learning has occurred for Jill, at this stage it is NOT complete. Too often, we find ourselves making the same mistakes and having to learn the same solutions over and over again. Just ask any coach and he or she will tell you that it takes a great deal of reinforcement and thus time, especially with brand new learning, to get them to stick. The root cause of this incomplete learning is that not enough has been done to reinforce the learning at the time it was best to reinforce it – which was during Pam's second session on the range.

Applying the 7-7 Rule

The 7-7 Rule states that in order to instill new learning, it has to be experienced in 7 different ways at 7 different times incorporating all the three research-based concepts of the 7-7 Rule. So for Pam, she has to consciously practice finishing her back swing to the top in 7 different ways at 7 different times (one of them being consciously doing it the old way to remind her to feel what she does not want to feel) to make sure her chances of not reverting to a shorter swing. As an example, here are Pam's 7-7 action steps:

1. Do 10 swings with focus on full back swing.
2. Do the 10 with a pause at the top to remind her to finish.
3. Purposefully swing with an incomplete backswing (negative reinforcement).
4. Have Jill verbally describe what she saw.
5. Practice consciously one swing correctly and another the 'old way' incorporating yellow card memories in between.
6. Tell at least 2 people about what you learned and did to fix your quick swing.
7. While laying in bed, visualize the practice session on the range and imagine all the movements as though you are there.

You can see Pam has incorporated all three concepts in her 7-7 Rule. She really wants to make sure she completes her back swing as it can cost her valuable strokes early in her round. Note also that many modalities and senses are being used. This method is allowing for imprinting of new neuropathways to re-direct the proverbial 'bad habits' which are nothing more than strongly entrenched neuropathways. The more senses are engaged in different modes in the imprinting process, the 7-7 process, then the more re-directing of old ways into new ones. This is a very different way of learning as most athletes focus purely on learning, and either not on imprinting that learning or using 'volume' or repetition for that imprinting. The latter is a very poor and inefficient way to imprint your learning, but used by many golfers simply because it 'seems' like the right thing to do.

Obviously, though these modalities worked for Pam, they may not work for you. You have to decide what you can do, based on your past positive learning, to make sure enough diversity is included that is personalized to your own style of learning to make it stick.

In proactive learning, which I recommend for ALL your sessions, it is much easier to implement both the learning methodology (i.e., the art and science of learning) and the 7-7 Rule if there actually is a purpose to your practice. Having a purpose almost always means having a way to measure your output. It can be distance, shot shape, spin, trajectory, etc. Hit a shot with a measurable desired output and use the result to see what can be learned. If you have a PURPOSE for your shot, then you are inherently opening yourself up to learning because if that purpose is not met, then the opportunity to apply the learning methodology and 7-7 rule also exists. Remember, you want to have these learning experiences in practice, not during a round where as described in Chapter 2, all the elements create a very non-conducive learning environment and quite frankly, there isn't enough logistical time or venue to practice different solutions to a problem you have never had before. Golfers that perform well talk of how slow everything goes, and conversely, those that do not, talk about how fast everything is. Time is neither faster nor slower – your thinking, dictated by your emotions, is. The cost of learning in a round can be very high as so many competing variables exist. This is why I recommend you truly embrace making mistakes – when you make them, learn from them. And if you do that, then you are preventing the prefrontal lobes from sounding a compromising alarm in your brain which dilutes your ability to make the right decision.

"Success does not consist in never making mistakes, but in never making the same one a second time" -George Bernard Shaw

Learning to Evaluate

I also recommend that every single practice session and round end with using the Goal Post Model.

Figure 9. The Goal Post

The Goal Post Model is quite simple. As you can see in the picture, the goal post looks like a football goal post. After every round, simply draw the goal post in your note book. Write down on the bottom left side of the post, just 1-3 things that went well in the round. On the bottom right side of the post, write 1-3 things that did not. Then on top of the goal post, notice three areas of space: inside the goal post, to the left of it and to the right of it.

Inside the goal post, in the middle, write down only 1-3 things from a golf skill perspective that you need to work on. On the left, write down only 1-3 things from a mental skill perspective that you need to work on – things like course management and decision-making. On the right, write down only 1-3 things from a EQ skill perspective that you need to work on – things like how often you felt yellow or red, whether you were present (next chapter) or how quickly or poorly you were able to get back to green.

Do this immediately after your round and consider the round not completed if this is not done. Review it just before your next practice whenever it may be. This model converts mundane and long practice and rounds into a learning activity, and allows you to have a goal for your next session. It is that simple.

In other professional sports, like say basketball, there is a sheet of paper that is printed and given to the coach at the end of each quarter that lists all the players who played, how many minutes they played, points scored, rebounds had, assists made, etc. This is used by the coaches to make adjustments and manage the game. Although golf is an individual sport, you need to also assess your performance and do the same thing in order to grow.

Complete Your Learning Template

Exercise: Learning Template

1. **Problem Statement:** _____

2. **Symptoms of Problem:**
   a. _____

   b. _____

   c. _____

3. **Potential Root Causes:**
   a. _____

   b. _____

   c. _____

4. Sources for Solution:

a._____

b._____

c._____

5. Potential Solutions:

a._____

b._____

c._____

As practice, apply the 7-7 rule to your solutions above:

1._____

2._____

3._____

4._____

5._____

6._____

7._____

Top 3 Ideas
I learned from this chapter
1.
2.
3.
3 Action Steps
I will take immediately to incorporate the above learning into my practice and rounds
1.
2.
3.

Chapter Summary

1. Being a proactive learner can significantly improve the quality of your practice on the range and rounds.
2. Learning takes place best when there is a purpose, and there is both an art and a science to it.
3. No round is complete without an evaluation of how you performed with golf skills, mental skills and emotional skills.
4. Everyone has a different learning style and should utilize that style to take advantage of opportunities.
5. Learning is only half of the equation to improvement. The other half is to make that learning stick by incorporating the 7-7 Rule.

Chapter 4

There has never been a shortage of ways to describe happiness. If we are lucky enough to have our basic needs (Maslow) of food, water, shelter and security met, then the pursuit of happiness comes into play. Because we have some form of "power" after meeting these basic needs – a purchasing power, a hierarchical power, a physical power, etc. – we want to naturally use that power to pursue or in most cases, purchase, happiness. The scientific studies and evidence correlating happy workers to productive workers and high degrees of innovation are abundant and at least 40 years old. There is indisputable evidence suggesting that happy workers or athletes outperform those who are not. It is, therefore, worth making happiness a workplace discussion topic. That is why it has been the most popular class at Harvard University. This is Part 1 of a 3 part Series on Happiness.

The first part is to offer a new definition. Perhaps one that is not philosophical, though admittedly those definitions have a valuable place in the discussion, but one more based on actual neuroscience. Our body is over 90% fluid. It is essentially a chemical factory constantly changing its composition based on the stimuli we receive, which then dictates the quality of cognitive discourse we have with ourselves and others, and behaviors we subsequently exhibit. To make it simple for the purposes of a short blog, let us say there are two dominant chemicals – one fills us with fear (cortisol) and another with happiness (dopamine). Factually, when fear is present in our physiological system, then our cognitive functions diminish, and countless biological functions are triggered to help us "just survive" the experience. Some of these experiences can result in permanent trauma, but most are of the kind that keep repeating themselves causing the same effects of trauma, leading to unhappiness and under-performance – never reaching our potential. Neurologically, let us define happiness as simply the absence of fear.

One key distinction to make before concluding is the difference between happy moments and happiness. They are not the same. Buying the car of your dreams is a happy moment as is eating your favorite dish or visiting your favorite place or getting a big bonus or winning a big event. Unless these moments directly result in removing fear, they are not happiness. I am making the argument that in pursuit of happiness, it is in fact not happiness that we need to pursue, but the removal of fear. When I work with professional athletes and ask them to describe a time when they played in that elusive state of being in a zone, when everything seems to go well, and feels effortless, they all describe attributes of what is ultimately a state without any fear.

This week, think about defining and redefining happiness for yourself. Consider my points above and discuss it with your spouses, loved ones, friends and, dare I say, workplace colleagues.

https://izzyjustice.wordpress.com/2015/02/15/happiness-part-1/

Happiness & Focus

You have been introduced to several concepts so far, most notably, that of how your brain makes decisions, Golf EQ, and learning. You now have several tools to incorporate into your practice sessions on the range or short game area. In the next four chapters, I will spend time on pre-round, during the round and post-round strategies, where it matters the most. But before I go there, in this chapter I will discuss two other key concepts of high performance not just in golf, but also in life: happiness and focus. A round of golf day lasts just a few hours, but your preparation for it and life itself consumes countless hours of both actual time and emotional energy that unequivocally come into play during your round. Practicing EQ during practice and life creates new neuropathways that during your round, when you need them most, will not be new. Your round should not be the place to try something new.

In the last chapter, you learned about how to learn to avoid those 'garbage' hours on the range or playing, where you are simply going through the motions and nothing is being learned, or worse, nothing is being imprinted. You may be doing it just to say you spent hours on the range to feel good. These "garbage" hours can be further reduced significantly by incorporating EQ in life itself, totally outside of golf.

Happiness

This is quite possibly the least considered variable in all of human performance, not just in athletic or golf performance. Some of you are no doubt skeptical here. You may ask 'what in the world does personal happiness have to do with a 3-foot putt?' and it is a fair question. It is infinitely more important, however, that you understand what happiness actually is, from a neuroscience perspective.

Some psychologists and philosophers argue that happiness is in fact, the ultimate pursuit. If you play golf, you do it to make yourself happy. If you work at an office, you do it to make money to do something to make you happy. If you play with your child, you do it to make you happy. If you listen to a song or read a book or watch a movie, at its core, you do it all because 'something' inside you makes you feel better. The clothes you chose to wear today, the way you do your hair, what you say – all of it – is an expression of your identity that you hope will either make you directly happy or accepted by others which itself would make you happy. These are activities that chase the dopamine hormone.

Another way to look at this ultimate pursuit is the converse. Who among you pursues activities that make you unhappy? It could even be argued that we intentionally avoid experiences that we know will make us unhappy. So clearly there is a ying-yang effect here of things that we do or happen to us that either make us happy or unhappy. Some of these things we choose, but many others we do not choose. You can choose to hug your child, but you cannot choose when someone screams at you.

There are countless stories of great athletes who suddenly look like they are clueless while performing, only to later find out that they just lost a loved one a day earlier or a similar personal tragedy. In professional golf, it is not hard to see a decline in performance when a negative life event, like a divorce or break-up, occurs. On the other hand, it is also noted that average golfers suddenly perform great when 'their personal life' gets in order. In either case, and so many in between the spectrum of something good or bad experiences of life, the golfers weight, IQ or golf swing does change and is impacted by those experiences.

List a time in your life when a negative experience impacted you negatively.

_____

_____

_____

List a time in your life when a positive experience impacted you positively.

_____

_____

_____

You are encouraged to complete the exercises above before proceeding so that what is next can be personal to you.

It is critical for those who seek higher performance to understand the role of happiness in their lives and performance.

The Neuroscience of Happiness

The human body is over 90% fluid. We are essentially a chemical factory with many hormones in our body released from several glands that determine what the composition of 'you' is at any given time. The chemical composition of the mix of hormones is constantly changing, mostly without your control or knowledge. You only find out after the fact by noticing the impact of the new chemical state.

Without giving you all a dissertation, let me simplify it down to two dominant families of hormones: Dopamine and Cortisol. Dopamine is your happy family of hormones and Cortisol is your unhappy family of hormones.

A good question to ask is why, if the ultimate pursuit is happiness, does the cortisol family even exist? Think back to the car coming at you in Chapter 2. In addition, the pursuit of happiness is a very new phenomenon in our evolution as human beings. We were built, as all living creatures are, to primarily defend ourselves and live to survive another day. We were designed so that if we saw a fire on our right, we would immediately, as described in Chapter 2 with the car, turn to our left and run. The same applies to seeing a lion coming at us to eat us, and running the opposite way or figuring out a way to fight it. Until the last 100 years or so, most human beings never traveled more than 50 miles of their place of birth nor lived beyond the age of 40. Our inherent design is not conducive to consistent high performance as that usually means we have to deal with failures constantly. This all happens because of the cortisol family of hormones and, for the most part, we still very much need them to continue to survive.

When the cortisol levels are higher than the dopamine levels, then, generally speaking, we are unhappy. The neurological state of unhappiness is simply that – presence of cortisol over dopamine. New research is showing that four out of five Americans are permanently in this yellow state because of negative experiences in the past, near past or currently being experienced. It could have been a traumatic childhood experience, or something that happened in a round last week, or a current health issue with you or a loved one. These experiences release cortisol in your body which creates the stress levels that we call unhappiness. And as already discussed, the physical body in yellow or red state cannot perform optimally to hit a small white ball standing still with a club at 100 mph - where even a slight mis-hit can lead to a flawed shot.

"The biggest rival I had in my career was me." -Jack Nicklaus

Given that golf is a game of misses filled with more disappointments (negative experiences releasing cortisol), the physical body is then constantly compromised to hit a golf ball the way you are capable of. And this does not even take into account all that has happened to you in life before you started your round. The idea that happiness can counteract these negative experiences was first explored in performance in the 1920s in the Hawthorne Experiments—something worth googling.

The **Hawthorne studies**, which were conducted by Elton Mayo and Fritz Roethlisberger in the 1920s with workers at the **Hawthorne** plant of the Western Electric Company, were part of an emphasis on sociopsychological aspects of human behavior in organizations. They found that by simply making lights brighter, factory workers 'felt happy' and productivity increased. They played music and the same positive impact on performance resulted.

Since then, neuroscience has emerged to take observations by psychologists; and now be able to explain them using digital imaging of the brain during states of happiness and unhappiness. An incredible amount of new research over the past decade has provided priceless knowledge on how to be happy.

Matt Killingsworth, a Harvard researcher, unveiled a great study on the correlation of happiness to being present. **He essentially showed that most human beings have their mind wondering 60% of the time.** In other words, 60% of the time, your mind is somewhere other than where you physically are, thinking about something else than what you are actually doing.

For golfers, and athletes in general, this is a very troubling statistic and explains "bubba golf" – where hitting the same shot the second time from the same place usually is better than the original one. In the second one, you are more 'present' than the first. It cannot possibly be a golf skill issue or mental issue because if it were, you would not be able to execute your second shot perfectly.

It is part of golf vernacular to hear 'stay in the present' or 'stay in the moment' but rarely has this been decoded with neuroscience, and even rarer, is how to do it beyond just telling someone to do it.

How to be Mindful – Stay in the Moment

"Concentration is a fine antidote to anxiety." -Jack Nicklaus

For the next section, you will need to be very disciplined and follow the instructions very carefully, exactly as prescribed otherwise you will compromise your own learning. You will need a picture of anything – a person or a place – and something you can eat like a fruit or power bar of some kind.

Being mindful or being in the present means that your neuropathways (thinking) are all correct in accessing the right memories and skills for the moment required.

We know that our thinking is a consequence of our emotions (Chapter 2) which, in turn, is a reaction to stimuli. So all the changes to that chemical composition of that 90% chemical factory, called the human body, begin with stimuli. Earlier, we learned to trick (self- stimulate) the brain with past positive experiences with the yellow and green cards. In the present moment, however, a different way can be used and it is complementary to the cards.

Stimuli enter our cognitive space in only five ways – sight, sound, smell, taste and feel. All stimuli must go through these channels to have meaning of any kind. To be present, to be in the moment, to be mindful, therefore, is having strong skills with these five sensory channels. It sounds bizarre at first pass to suggest that you are going to learn to see, or hear, or taste, or smell or feel – we have been doing this since we were born. But how many of you have actually been taught to enhance these skills?

We know people who are blind who have unbelievable hearing skills, but no biological reason for that enhanced hearing skill. They have simply trained themselves to be better at hearing as a necessity. We may also know people who are deaf but have incredible sense of feel and sight, yet no biological reason for that other than training themselves to be better at them. The point here is that having a better skill over your entry senses is very much possible and you have simply not explored it because you have not had the need to or do not know how to do it. You will learn now.

Sight

I will start with the most powerful of the five senses – sight. Take the picture you were asked to have and look at it.

Write down three unique attributes of what you see in that picture:

1. _____
2. _____
3. _____

Look at the picture again now, and write down three additional attributes of what you see in that picture:

4. _____
5. _____
6. _____

Look at the picture again now, and write down three additional attributes of what you see in that picture:

7. _____
8. _____
9. _____

Look at the picture again now, and write down three additional attributes of what you see in that picture:

10. _____
11. _____
12. _____

Look at the picture again now, and write down three additional attributes of what you see in that picture:

13. _____
14. _____
15. _____

If you completed each set of the above exercise, you are probably surprised as you thought you could not come up with new unique attributes.

"You can see a lot by just looking." -Yogi Berra

If you went further, you could probably come up with another 15. One of the best ways to practice this is to look at the live face of a loved one – a spouse or child - and come up with 50 unique attributes of his or her face only. It is an advanced skill, but can easily be done with any face. You will find yourself noticing every little feature. And in that moment of looking and searching, your mind is in no other place than the present. **This is how you use sight to stay present**. This is how you use sight to focus - which I will discuss at length later in this chapter. Just imagine ALL the things that are available to the eye during a round of golf that you simply do not notice. If you can pick out 15 attributes in just one picture, and be present, how many could you pick up on each hole, that could equally keep your mind from wandering and be in the present?

Sound

The next most powerful of the five senses is sound. For this, just stay wherever you are reading this book and close your eyes before each set and zone in on just listening.

Close your eyes and hear three unique sounds wherever you presently are. Write them down below:

1. _____
2. _____
3. _____

Close your eyes again and hear three additional unique sounds wherever you presently are. Write them down below:

4. _____
5. _____
6. _____

Close your eyes again and hear three additional unique sounds wherever you presently are. Write them down below:

    7. _____
    8. _____
    9. _____

Close your eyes again and hear three additional unique sounds wherever you presently are. Write them down below:

    10. _____
    11. _____
    12. _____

Close your eyes again and hear three additional unique sounds wherever you presently are. Write them down below:

    13. _____
    14. _____
    15. _____

If you completed each set of the above exercise, you are probably surprised as you thought you could not come up with new unique sounds.

"You can win tournaments when you're mechanical, but golf is a game of emotion and adjustment. If you're not aware of what's happening to your mind and your body when you're playing, you'll never be able to be the very best you can be." -Jack Nicklaus

If you went further, you could probably come up with more sounds. This is an advanced skill but can easily be done by practicing literally anywhere, at any time. Eventually, you will find yourself noticing every little sound the way perhaps a skilled blind person does. And in that moment of listening and searching for new sounds, your mind is in no other place than the present. **This is how you use sound to stay present.** This is how you use sound to focus, which I will discuss at length later in this chapter. Just imagine ALL the things that are available to hear during a round of golf that you simply do not choose to hear. If you can pick out 15 sounds just where you are now, and be present, how many could you pick up on each hole, that could equally keep your mind from wandering and be in the present?

Feel

Next is feel. Like sound, just stay wherever you are reading this book and close your eyes before each set and zone in on just feeling something on your body.

Close your eyes and feel three unique sensations all over your body wherever you presently are. Write them down below:

1. _____
2. _____
3. _____

Close your eyes and feel three additional unique sensations all over your body wherever you presently are. Write them down below:

4. _____
5. _____
6. _____

Close your eyes and feel three additional unique sensations all over your body wherever you presently are. Write them down below:

7. _____
8. _____
9. _____

Close your eyes and feel three additional unique sensations all over your body wherever you presently are. Write them down below:

10. _____
11. _____
12. _____

Close your eyes and feel three additional unique sensations all over your body wherever you presently are. Write them down below.

13. _____
14. _____
15. _____

If you completed each set of the above exercise, you are probably surprised as you thought you could not come up with new unique sensations to feel.

If you went further, you could probably come up with another 15. This is not an advanced skill and can be practiced anywhere anytime. You will find yourself feeling everything on you perhaps even the sweat on your head when playing. And in that moment of feeling and searching, your mind is in no other place than the present. **This is how you use feel to stay present.** This is how you use feel to focus, which I will discuss at length later in this chapter. Just imagine ALL the things that are available to feel during a round of golf that you simply do not notice. Perhaps it's the glove, or your grip or a towel or the dimples on the ball in your hand. If you can pick out 15 attributes in just where you are now, and be present, how many could you pick up on each hole, that could equally keep your mind from wandering and be in the present?

Taste

The next sense is taste. For this, you will need that power bar mentioned earlier. For this, just stay wherever you are reading this book and close your eyes before each set and zone in on just tasting.

Close your eyes and take a small bite of whatever you have and eat it the way you would normally eat and notice three unique tastes of what you ate. Write them down below:

1. _____
2. _____
3. _____

Close your eyes again, take another bite and taste three additional unique tastes. Write them down below:

4. _____
5. _____
6. _____

If you completed each set of the above exercise, you are probably surprised as you thought you could not come up with new unique tastes.

If you went further, you could probably come up with more tastes in flavor or texture or the way it sits in your mouth. This is an advanced skill but can easily be done by practicing literally anywhere, at any time and especially when you eat – which for most of us is at least three times a day. Why not practice this every single time you eat? Eventually, you will find yourself noticing every little taste, the way perhaps a skilled person like a sommelier does. And in that moment of tasting and searching for new tastes, your mind is in no other place than the present. **This is how you use taste to stay present.** This is how you use taste to focus, which I will discuss at length later in this chapter. Just imagine ALL the things that are available to taste during a round of golf that you simply do not choose to taste from what you drink and eat. Why waste that experience since you have to do it anyway? If you can pick out six tastes just with one type of food, and be present, how many could you pick up on each hole if you tasted what you drank or ate, that could equally keep your mind from wandering and be in the present?

Smell

This is difficult to do in book format, and in a room or house. It is best to practice this when outside at a restaurant or outdoor event. Do the same thing as the previous four and close your eyes and seek out three new smells at a time till you get to 12. When playing golf, as you approach the clubhouse on the 9th or 18th holes, if you engage your sense of smell, you can pick up many smells. In a PGA Tour event where there are concession stands on every hole just about, it is even easier to engage the sense of smell. And again, by engaging in this sense, you are focusing your mind to respond to the present moment, not wander and give you a path to lower cortisol by allowing dopamine levels to increase.

What is critical to understand is that being in the moment is a function of your senses. Engaging your sensory organs in this manner allows you to not wander, which, according to Killingsworth's research, is the most powerful way to be happy in any given moment.

This is the same physiological mechanism in play when you are on vacation. Often times, you will go to a place like the beach or mountains. You find that relaxing. The reason is that your senses, all of them, are experiencing a heightened engagement because of the uniqueness of the stimuli of the environment. In other words, the exercises that were just done above with the five senses are happening naturally. Your eyes are looking at the beach, hearing the sounds of the waves, feeling the salty breeze that is common in ocean air. All these cause you to be present, thinking of what you are experiencing instead of what happened the week before or what needs to happen when you return.

The same is said of artists who go to places to search for inspiration. They might go to a cabin in the mountains, for example. The view of trees, greenery, air, natural sounds all do the same thing for the artist. They keep him present and happy allowing him to write the lyrics to the song, or paint, or write a book.

What is important to understand is that the inspiration or happiness is happening because senses are engaged fully, and going to a far-away location is a good way of doing it, but by no means the only way. It is possible to be that mindful and inspired wherever you are if you can learn to engage with your senses. The golf course, a place that is often manicured perfectly with large fairways, trees, flowers, ponds, lakes, rivers, and such, is in fact one of the best places to engage with your senses. It is a huge advantage over, say basketball, where it is always indoors with a sea of fans around or other sporting events that are stadium-style.

It is impossible, and not necessary, to be a perfectly happy person to perform at a high level; but it is necessary to be able to use your senses to be exactly where you need to be while playing golf so that your negative life experiences do not compromise your ability to execute the shot you are capable of. Being mindful, being present while playing golf, by using these techniques is the most effective way to suspend some of life challenges and concurrently manage your neuropathways and chemical composition to allow you to bring out the best you've got.

"Every great player has learned the two C's: how to concentrate and how to maintain composure." -Byron Nelson

FOCUS

Being mindful in the manner described allows you to be focused at the task at hand, and not on the past or future but in the present moment. Focus is the term often used to describe a golfer who is playing in a zone, executing every shot physically, mentally and emotionally to the best ability.

Once present, there are additional ways to complement the senses that are more mental in order to be even further focused with your shot. Being mindful can allow these focal thoughts to be very powerful tools to use during your round.

1. SKILL FOCAL THOUGHT

Once you are in the moment, then it is time to work on building your focus skills and becoming a better golfer.

A focal thought is one specific golf skill-based form or technique that you can use in your practice or a round. For example, it might be to 'grip lightly', or 'release-putter', or 'finish backswing.' Whatever the skill focal point is, it must be very directly related to something you are working on. It usually is a thought that helps you remember something that you are just learning or often forget to do. Every practice must have at least one skill focal thought. It should be used throughout your practice, and this is where your ability to focus (macro and micro) can really help you master this skill focal thought.

> **Write down some specific Skill Focal Thought (SFT) for your round next week:**
>
> **Swing Focal Thought:**_____
>
> **Putting Focal Thought:**_____
>
> **Pre shot Focal Thought:**_____

"All that we are is the result of what we have thought." -Buddha

2. EQ FOCAL THOUGHT

Similar to the skill focal thought, an EQ focal thought is much simpler. It is an EMOTIONAL focal thought. It usually is just one word or a very short phrase for that specific round, like a mantra. Its purpose is to get you to relax and even enjoy your round. It may be the name of your collegiate mascot, your favorite pro golfer, your favorite course, your spouse or children, your favorite color, or anything that works for you. The purpose of your EQ Focal thought is to have an operating mantra for the entire round no matter what happens. Your ability to revisit this mantra is a measure of your mindfulness and emotional strength. Catch yourself forgetting it. Change it up for each round or practice session.

Make a list of all the EQ Focal Thoughts that come to mind and use them for your next round:

a. _____

b. _____

c. _____

d. _____

e. _____

f. _____

g. _____

h. _____

i. _____

j. _____

"Confidence in golf means being able to concentrate on the problem at hand with no outside interference." -Tom Watson

3. MACRO FOCUS

Macro focus is an emotionally light way to stay present using your senses as described earlier. It may be to notice the trees, clouds, wind, lawns, ponds, flowers, and such. Macro focus is the type of focus required as soon as you enter the golf course property. Once you pass the gate of the entrance of the golf course, you are now a golfer. You are no longer all your other roles in life.

A fundamental premise in focus is that a conscious effort to think about one thing is a subconscious effort to not think about another thing.

If you choose to notice the big oak tree by the gate of the entrance of the golf course, you are subconsciously choosing to not think about the work you have just left or have to do afterwards. You can use all your senses to macro focus. It is important to keep this focus light and make sure it is not the type that drains you emotionally or mentally. It can be smelling the hamburgers being grilled, the shape of clouds, the feel of wind on your body, or hearing birds chirp. This is all light and allows you to be present as described earlier.

During the round, macro focus should be the exclusive focus between all shots with the only exception being when you have hit an undesired shot where you will need to breathe and rely on your yellow or red cards. This should complement your EQ focal thought and go hand-in-hand to manage the cortisol and dopamine battle going on in your body.

"Everything was fine, until I walked onto the first tee!" -Seve Ballesteros

4. MICRO FOCUS

Micro focus is different from macro focus in that micro is a much deeper focus, not light at all. It is a laser-type of focus on a very specific task or spot. Because it is heavier, it is only recommended once you are over the ball. An example is to use sight skills to notice not the ball you are about to strike, but a very specific dimple where you want the club face to hit it. It might also be to feel the grip in every part of your hand and fingers, or to feel your feet in shoes sensing every inch of the ground underneath. It can even be to sense the saliva in your mouth or quality of air going into your mouth and lungs. When you are over the ball, about to strike, that is the time when all the focus has to be on the shot needed to be executed and nothing else. Not what happened on the last shot, last week, what is happening at home, or whatever else negative is in your life. Thus, micro focus using the techniques of mindfulness to make you the happiest, and in the most present of states to do just that.

It is imperative that you not start micro focus until you are really over the ball about to hit it. Using micro focus between shots will deplete your emotional energy and you will be exhausted before the round is up. Between shots is when to use macro focus, the light mindfulness technique to still be present.

Top 3 Ideas
I learned from this chapter
1.
2.
3.
3 Action Steps
I will take immediately to incorporate the above learning into my practice and rounds
1.
2.
3.

"Tell me and I forget, teach me and I may remember, involve me and I learn." -Benjamin Franklin

Chapter Summary

1. Happiness is a chemical state dictated by the battle between the family of hormones of cortisol (fear) and dopamine.
2. Being present or mindful is a neurologically proven technique to be happy in the moment, increasing dopamine over cortisol and allowing your body to mentally recall a skill and physically execute a shot.
3. The five senses are an under-utilized asset that, when used to be present, can allow for powerful ways to focus.
4. The golf course is a great place to engage all your senses to be mindful, an advantage over other sports.
5. There are skill focus thoughts, EQ focal thoughts, macro and micro focus that collectively can form a powerful emotional strength framework to get you to perform at your best.

Chapter 5

Whether I am coaching an executive in a company or a professional athlete, I always ask the question: What is your Passion Statement? The answer can't be "because I love what I do." The answer should be why you love what you do. What is it about what you do that you find meaningful? How much of the response is really a part of your identity?

Unlike elevator speeches, which are those 60-second pitches describing who you are or what you do, the primary audience for Passion Statements is yourself. It should not be what you think someone else wants to hear, or what you are supposed to say because of what you do. Passion Statements are truthful descriptors of yourself and invaluable to revisit frequently as you struggle to maintain passion for what you do. Passion, by definition, is that often indescribable, very envious and very explicit emotional condition that reveals your Passion Statement. You can see it in an athlete who has it and in one who does not, and the same goes for people we work with. We love people with passion behind what they do. For them, it does not ever look like work.

This week, take time to craft your passion statement. At the end of the week, take inventory of your actions and see if your behavior reflected your Passion Statement. If it did, you likely had a great week. If it did not, it was probably a tough week. Make adjustments and align your passion statement to your actions. You will 'work' less and get more by doing so!

https://izzyjustice.wordpress.com/2015/07/05/passion-statements/

Phases of Golf

In the next three chapters, all the concepts discussed in previous chapters will be put into a very real model of how all golfers should manage themselves in a logical sequence to perform at high levels. Within each of these phases, tools that have been discussed in previous chapters will be brought together in a real applicable way.

There is an additional premise in all of sports, but especially in golf, that every professional athlete is aware of—that is, preparation for competition must include a plan for unplanned mishaps. Preparing for a round as though everything is going to go well, or not having a plan if things do not go well, is a recipe for disaster. Making it up during competition by relying on your memory, as already discussed in previous chapters, is leaving too many items to chance. That preparation is not just with the physical game of golf, but with the mental and emotional parts of it too. Great athletes do not want to leave their performance and their success to chance. They want to be prepared for all outcomes, positive and negative ones, planned and unplanned ones. When an athlete is surprised by a situation, and guesses on how to effectively respond, that is a sign of poor preparation. Many professional golfers will intentionally plug their balls in the bunker for example, as that is preparing for something that could happen. By hitting a plugged lie, they are preparing physically for a shot they did not plan for. The same approach should be taken emotionally and mentally.

"We create success or failure on the course primarily by our thoughts." -Gary Player.

Below are the phases that require all three skills. It is a sequence of all the steps before and after a round of golf that you need to perform at your best.

Sequence of Golf

Practice	EQ & Mental Taper	Warm-up	Competitive Round	Goal Post	Refill EQ Tank	Practice

Figure 10. Sequence of Golf

It starts with practice. You probably go to the range or short game area and work on your swing and several short shots. This is where most of the preparation for that competitive round of golf takes place. This is necessary, but only one of the many pieces required for high performance.

The 2nd phase in the sequence is EQ and Mental preparation. This should take place 1-3 days before your competitive round of golf and will be discussed at length later.

The 3rd phase is during the day of competition – your key round. This includes a warm-up strategy, strategy for your round; and as discussed earlier, no round should be complete without the Goal Post evaluation, which should occur immediately after the round.

The last phase is refilling EQ, which needs to occur within 1-3 days after that round if it is a single competitive round. If there is a consecutive round on the next day, then it needs to happen once you leave the course until you re-enter it the next day. The completion of the tournament or round then leads you back to where you start again, which is practice.

Let us review each phase.

Practice

Practice	EQ & Mental Taper	Warm-up	Competitive Round	Goal Post	Refill EQ Tank	Practice

Figure 11. Phase: Practice

Key points for practice have already been discussed in previous chapters, but here they are again:

1. All your practice must have a purpose. The human brain, much to our chagrin, can only learn about one meaningful golf skill at a time. So pick only one purpose for each session on the range. Any session more than three hours greatly diminishes the brain's capacity to learn something new because of fatigue - physical, mental and emotional - as competing neuropathways are now able to be more powerful than a new one.
2. Once you have achieved that goal, that purpose of practice, the entire focus should shift immediately into the 7-7 imprinting mode. This could happen after the first swing where something 'clicked' or after the 100th swing. Whenever it happens, you run a significant probability of actually losing that 'aha' if you keep practicing it (repetition) or decide to go work on something else. Shift to 7-7 quickly.
3. Use the Learning Template (root cause analysis) when you hit shots that just do not make sense to you. Use it often so that when it comes to using it after the round, you have built a strong skill in evaluation as you will likely be your own coach in many a situation and you will need a tool to process your performance.
4. Before going to the range, practice your macro focus once you enter the golf course property and measure a big part of your success at the range on how present you are.

5. Use macro focus between shots even though the time between shots will be significantly less than the time between shots during a round. Perhaps you want to look at a cloud or a nearby house and notice 10 unique attributes of it before hitting the next shot.
6. Use micro focus on every shot and try different ones per shot. On one shot it could be feeling the grip, on another it could be picking a dimple on the ball or feeling the ground underneath you.
7. Take your emotional temperature after every shot. Is it green, yellow or red? If it is anything but green, practice your breathing and cards. Remember that practicing while yellow or red is 'garbage' and likely to do more harm than good.
8. Visualize your shots by visualizing the best shot you have hit with the club in your hands instead of visualizing how you want the ball to go. That is, leverage the power of an existing memory as opposed to a non-existent future one.
9. Have a fun section for your practice. Hit at least five balls trying something totally new. Perhaps you saw a pro hit a shot on TV that was really impressive, like Bubba Watson's 100 yard hook shot with a wedge to win the masters.
10. End all practice making sure you are in a positive mental and emotional state. Mentally, you feel like you are thinking positively and are able to process data points to make good decisions. Emotionally, you should feel like something positive happened that you can leverage should you have to go play a round the next day.

3 Action Steps

I will take immediately to incorporate the above learning into my practice

1.
2.

3.

"The more I practice, the luckier I get." -Gary Player.

EQ & IQ Taper

Practice	EQ & Mental Taper	Warm-up	Competitive Round	Goal Post	Refill EQ Tank	Practice

Figure 12. Phase: EQ & Mental Taper

Tapering is a concept of winding-down to prepare for the competitive round, the round that really matters where you have to perform at a high level. During this phase, the focus on golf skills needs to diminish each day and, concurrently, the focus on EQ and IQ needs to increase each day leading up to game day.

In the 1-3 days leading up to your big round, substitute the physical training time with EQ training time. If you are up at night and not sleeping, then work on your EQ. Here are some things you can do several days prior to round:

1. Practice taking your EQ temperature every hour.
2. Make current your YELLOW and RED cards.
3. Practice using your cards.
4. Engage in conversation with people who you know will be encouraging and have positive dialogues.
5. View every experience as one that can make you GREEN or YELLOW. By taking your temperature, proactively steer yourself toward GREEN experiences and steer away from YELLOW experiences.
6. Fine tune your suggested monologues for the round – and practice them on your taper days.

7. Begin Macro Focus through the week so that on game day, you are already used to it.
8. On the night before the round, if you are not sleeping, then instead of letting your thoughts wander, engage in very strong visualization exercises where you recall past good rounds or past positive experiences of your life (in sport or life in general).
9. Also, if you get up very early and want to do something, then practice light meditative yoga, using very low intensity poses in conjunction with light soothing music, and practice A and C breathing in the ACT Breathing Model.
10. The golden EQ rule is to engage in positive activities, the kinds that make you feel very good about yourself, cause you to smile, laugh, and be joyful.

Fill EQ Tank during Tapering

One reason that tapering is so difficult for many is that it is emotionally counter-intuitive to slow down days before a big round or tournament, especially when you are used to hitting so many balls and spending so much time on the golf course. The goal is to start your round day with your EQ tank full and almost overflowing with positive feelings and thoughts.

This means to associate yourself with people, in activities, and in experiences that are very positive and encouraging. It also means to consciously avoid people and experiences that can be EQ depleting.

Reduce Golf Activity

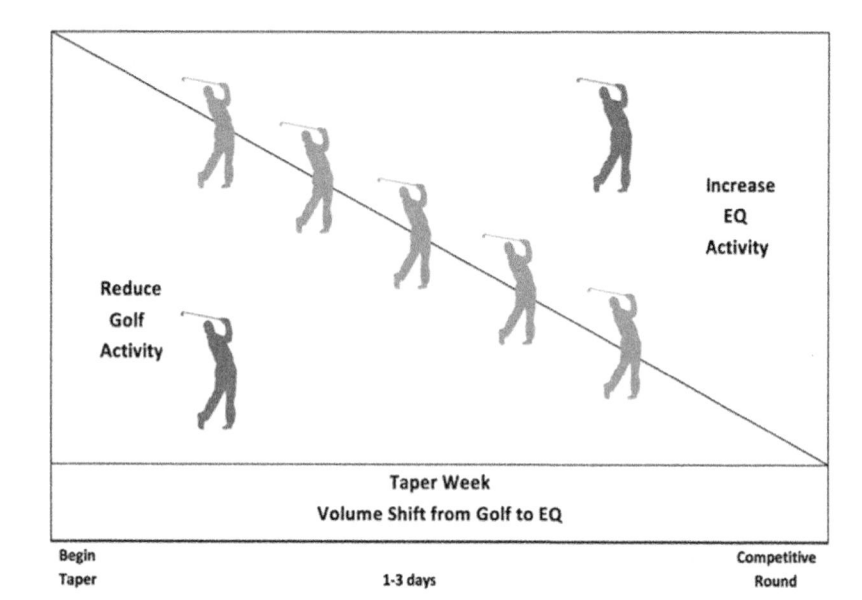

Increase EQ Activity

Taper Week
Volume Shift from Golf to EQ

Begin Taper — 1-3 days — Competitive Round

Figure 13. Tapering

> Make a list of 10 Activities you can do during Taper days that can fill your EQ Tank. These can be anything from watching your favorite movies, reading inspiring books, eating foods you love, talking to people who will be supportive, etc.
>
> 1. _____
> 2. _____
> 3. _____
> 4. _____
> 5. _____
> 6. _____
> 7. _____
> 8. _____
> 9. _____
> 10. _____

> Make a list of 5 Activities to avoid during Taper days. You know from past experiences that these will deplete your EQ Tank. These can be anything from negative people in your life, to activities that are stressful or events that require significant amount of your EQ.
>
> 1. _____
> 2. _____
> 3. _____
> 4. _____
> 5. _____

Emotional nourishment during taper days sets the stage for high EQ during the round as you now know that golf is a game of mishaps and each mishap will release cortisol that will direct your thoughts to negative ones, depleting you of EQ. So filling up the EQ tank is critical. In addition, it addresses so many very manageable pre-round anxieties.

Remember, your round does not really start until something goes wrong. That is when the real tournament and battle begins.

"It's never easy to win but it's a lot easier to win when you play well. The key is winning tournaments when you are not playing so well."
-Rory McLlory

All great athletes have a plan for what will go wrong. A golf (skill) plan, an EQ and a Mental plan.

Below is a list of very common mishaps that can happen before a round. Regrettably, one or more of these will likely happen to you on your round. It is better to have thought through how you will address the calamity beforehand, during training. As you review this list, make a note of how you will address them if they were to occur to you. You may already know how to address some of them, but may not know how to address others. The only way to know for sure that you are prepared is to address them in practice rounds. If you do not have the knowledge or skill to address the issue, then work with your coach, peers, golf professionals, or seek information from the internet (YouTube is an excellent source of "how to" information) and try it in practice. Your candor in this exercise will only serve you well.

Potential Pre-Round Mishaps

1. Fatigue due to over training (too much time on golf) or anxiety.
2. Fatigue due to lack of sleep.
3. Upset stomach.
4. Inability to have a good pre-round meal.
5. Worrying about having all the right equipment.
6. Realize you have forgotten/lost an important piece of equipment.
7. Late for the round.
8. Unable to go to the bathroom at golf course.
9. A loved one is in dire circumstance.
10. Feeling stiff, forget to stretch or warm up before round.
11. Did not prepare for changes in weather (rain, colder or warmer than forecasted, etc.).
12. Getting stung by a critter.

"Success is going from failure to failure, without loss of enthusiasm."
– Winston Churchill.

Make a list of 10 pre-round mishaps that could happen to you in the days leading to a tournament. For each one, think of a solution. Then, during training, purposefully induce one or more of these mishaps and see if your solution would work.

1. Mishap: _____
   _____

   Solution: _____
   _____
   _____

2. Mishap: _____
   _____

   Solution: _____
   _____
   _____

3. Mishap: _____
   _____

   Solution: _____
   _____
   _____

4. Mishap: _____
   _____

   Solution: _____
   _____
   _____

5. Mishap: _____

Solution: _____

6. Mishap: _____

Solution: _____

7. Mishap: _____

Solution: _____

8. Mishap: _____

Solution: _____

9. Mishap: _____

Solution: _____

10. Mishap: _____

_____

Solution: _____

_____

_____

The easiest way to not forget something is to make a list. Period. You should create your own tournament check list with your coach, caddie, or by yourself.

Mental Preparation

This is different from golf preparation and EQ preparation. As noted earlier, you are going to have to process hundreds of data points to make many decisions. Mental preparation includes a course management strategy of how you will play each hole and then deviate from that Plan A if conditions or circumstances change.

For each hole you must have an idea of what club you want to hit, and where you want the ball to end, so that you can best attack the green or pin position. This will differ for each hole, each golf course, and even each day when conditions often change. Write down this strategy in your yardage book along with a Plan B. There are numerous resources already available to help you do this. As such, this book will defer to those subject matter experts.

> **Make a list of 10 mental activities you can do during Taper days to prepare for your round.**
>
> 1. _____
> 2. _____
> 3. _____
> 4. _____
> 5. _____
> 6. _____
> 7. _____
> 8. _____
> 9. _____
> 10. _____

Fatigue

Fatigue on game day can occur for many reasons. The physical impact on the body due to fatigue is very powerful. Fatigue is a major trigger for our friend, Cortisol. Negativity will result as these hormones will force you to want to rest up by inducing all kinds of negativity and self-doubt.

Fatigue can set in because of lack of sleep during the nights leading up to your round. Though common, this, too, is a manageable challenge. The anxiety of a round is very real. It is filled with excitement, the presence of so many other golfers in the area or at your hotel, and the anxiety that all your practice will now be tested. This is all EQ related. Thus, the criticality of taper days.

Top 3 Ideas
I learned from this chapter
1.
2.
3.
3 Action Steps
I will take immediately to incorporate the above learning into my practice and taper days
1.
2.
3.

Chapter Summary

1. No matter how well prepared, both amateurs and professional golfers will experience some form of a mishap during a competitive round which is when the tournament really begins. What separates you from the competition is how you handle it.
2. It is common to feel anxiety during your taper days. A good practice to help alleviate this anxiety and fill the void left by your decreased golf training load is to increase your EQ activities as you want to enter the round with an overflowing EQ Tank.
3. Thinking through each potential mishap in advance and having a golf, EQ and mental plan is critical to avoid surprises during your round when everything seems to go very fast, and poor decisions can be made if you have not rehearsed mishaps.

Chapter 6

I want you to pick your competition for 2015. Go ahead – write it down. Who do you want to be better than in 2015? If your answer was another human being, then you have underperformed already- and arguably already lost.

Whoever you listed as your competition, they are the very people you have already given power over you. In your mind, you have convinced yourself that beating them is your success. What if you beat them when they were having an off-day? What if you beat them, but the price of that for you was a regret? What if you beat them, yet that point was still well below what you are capable of doing? What if you lose to them, but did your absolute best? What if you lose to them before it was really over and gave up? What if you lose to them and are much happier with your effort than they are with their victory? The answers to all these questions are a lot more complicated than if you simply changed who you decided were going to be your competition for 2015. What if your competition was a stretch goal for yourself – What if your goal was to be better than you have ever been at what you do? What if your goal was simply to get the most out of your mind, body and skills each day – to be able to look at yourself on your drive home and say, "I did my absolute best today. I gave it all I had. No regrets."

My argument is that you will undoubtedly go farther by making yourself your competition than by picking other people as your competition. This week, look around you and the people you work with or traditionally compete with, and take back the power you gave them – invest that energy instead in making yourself the absolute best on every single day in 2015.

https://izzyjustice.wordpress.com/2015/01/05/chose-your-2015-competition/

Warm Up

Practice	EQ & Mental Taper	Warm-up	Competitive Round	Goal Post	Refill EQ Tank	Practice

Figure 14. Phase: Warm Up

There are several parts to effectively warming up for a competitive round of golf. Most golfers will warm up by hitting several drives and then heading to the first.

Having a very structured plan for the warm up is critical so that all the skills that will be used and tested are warmed up.

There are four parts to the warm up that are recommended:

1. EQ
2. IQ (mental)
3. Golf
4. Physical

The warm up for EQ starts from the moment you enter the golf course property. Have a landmark like a gate at the entrance or the parking lot. From that moment until you leave the golf course, begin to slowly practice macro focus via your senses. Some athletes start even before that on their drive to the course by playing their favorite music in their cars or noticing clouds and trees on the drive. Remember, **a conscious effort to do this is a subconscious effort to not think of something else**, especially any negativity (cortisol) that might exist in your life. EQ preparation will be spread throughout the warm up.

According to my research, the optimal preparation time once on the golf course is about 90 minutes.

Recommended first is about a 20-minute physical warm up. This includes stretching and activating core muscles that will be used in your golf swing. Activating hips, glutes, back, chest, shoulders and arms with quick holds on each muscle is key to stretching out the muscles, allowing for warming of those muscles with increased blood flow. A yoga routine is a perfectly acceptable alternative also. Holding each pose with quick pulses has been proven to be excellent 'wake up' exercises.

You can also practice EQ during these stretches by closing your eyes and feeling each stretch at a specific point in the muscle. This is mindfulness practice incorporated into the physical warm up.

Next is about 45 minutes with golf. This should include a purposeful time with each shot in lieu of just hitting balls. It is recommended that the total number of balls hit during this golf warm up be about 50. This should encompass range time, short game time and putting. This will be roughly one ball per minute which will seem very slow to you - and that is intentional. The speed of the round (in your mind) will be much faster and the best place to slow it down is with the warm up. How many balls you hit with whatever club is your choice, and perhaps your coach can assist with the right ratio of balls per club.

The last 25 minutes should be spent on EQ and the mental game. Begin to take inventory of your thoughts. Are they positive or negative? What is your emotional temperature? Green, Yellow or Red? Review your cards and all your equipment with the primary goal being to walk to the first tee as green as possible.

"If there is one thing I have learned during my years as a professional, it is that the only thing consistent about golf is its inconsistency." -Jack Nicklaus

What is equally important in the warm-up is to manage mishaps. There are all kinds of mishaps that can happen just before your round. Not managed well, and you will be yellow or red going to the first tee, which is no good. Some of the mishaps were discussed in the last chapter, but additional ones are listed below.

Potential Warm-up Mishaps

1. Your driver is cracked.
2. Forgetting food or hydration.
3. Finding out your tee time has changed.
4. Paired with a negative player.
5. Paired with a slow or too fast player.
6. Forgetting to pack extra balls or gloves.
7. Greens appear faster/slower than day before.
8. You realize you are missing a club.
9. Weird cramp or other muscle issue.
10. They changed the tee boxes.

Make a list of 10 warm up mishaps that could happen to you just before your round. For each one, think of a solution. Then, during training, purposefully induce one or more of these mishaps and see if your solution would work.

1. Mishap:
_____
_____

Solution:_____
_____
_____

2. Mishap:
_____
_____

Solution:_____
_____
_____

3. Mishap:
_____
_____

Solution:_____
_____
_____

4. Mishap:
_____
_____

Solution:_____
_____
_____

5. Mishap: _____
   _____

   Solution: _____
   _____
   _____

6. Mishap: _____
   _____

   Solution: _____
   _____
   _____

7. Mishap: _____
   _____

   Solution: _____
   _____
   _____

8. Mishap: _____
   _____

   Solution: _____
   _____
   _____

9. Mishap: _____
   _____

   Solution: _____
   _____
   _____

> **10. Mishap:** _____
> _____
>
> **Solution:**_____
> _____
> _____

Remember, golf is a game of mishaps. Having a plan for what you want to do is great, but you must also have a plan for all the things that can go wrong. The previous chapters have given you specific skills to now be able to effectively do both during the warm up.

As you walk to the first tee, you are likely to feel a very normal sense of anxiety. Let us process how to incorporate an anxiety-reducing strategy - that walk.

"Aptitude starts with attitude." –Greg Norman

Anxiety

I have discussed how the brain works, the impact of a threatening stimulus and how it would cause your prefrontal lobes (threat center) to sound the "alarm" to your glands, thus disabling your brain and body. It is your perception of imminent threat that is at the heart of your anxiety. This results in going to those negative memories and monologues, like the stories shared in Chapter 1.

Figure 7 in Chapter 2 shows how your entire body reacts when in YELLOW, or under anxiety. One of the measurable symptoms is a very high heart rate (HR.) Research has shown that the first spike in anxiety (HR) is always the highest. This is why many times the walk to the first tee and the first tee shot tend to be difficult, from an EQ perspective. The graph below shows a normal anxiety pattern. Over time, after the initial shock of stimuli alerting you to the start of the round where shots suddenly matter, your brain slowly begins to note that nothing fatal has occurred and you can do this. Cortisol levels dilute with time. You begin to 'settle down', as they say. This is the case with all anxiety where the initial perceived threat, or sudden threat results, in huge spikes of cortisol and HR. As the round progresses, the threat subsides as your brain realizes you have made it and cortisol levels drops.

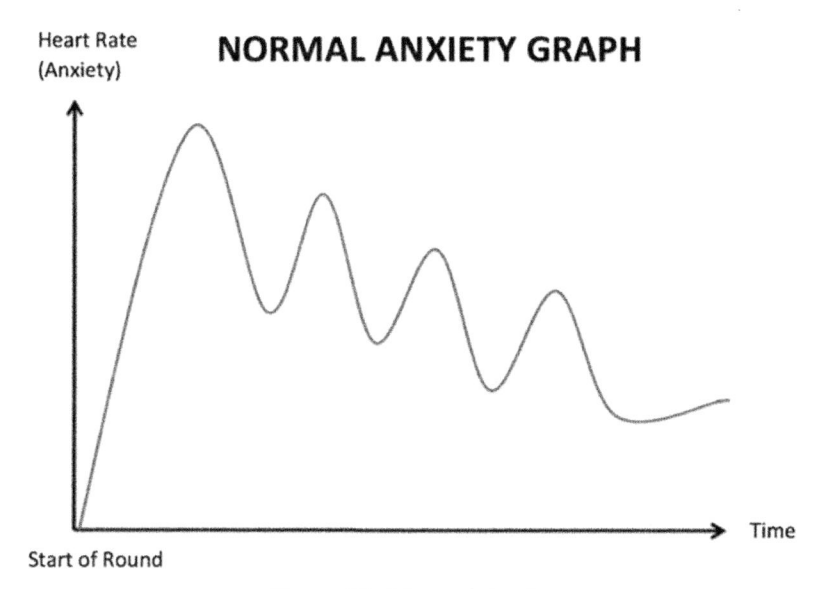

Figure 15. Normal Anxiety

As the round progresses, there may be additional HR spikes when a terrible or unexpected shot is experienced. Knowing that all of us are going to experience that initial spike in HR (although to varying degrees), one of the best ways to manage this first tee anxiety is to simulate the high HR just minutes before the start of the round. See the graph below:

MANAGED ANXIETY GRAPH

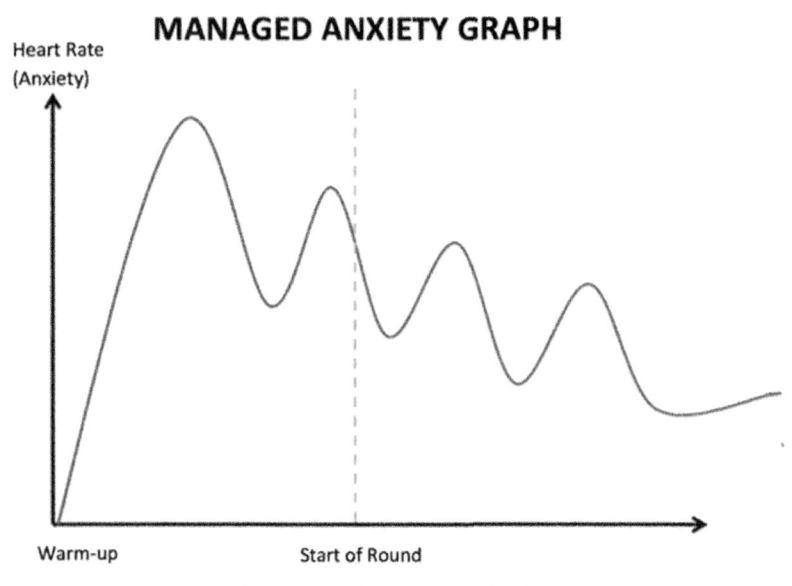

Figure 16. Managed Anxiety

In this graph, note that the anxiety levels are identical to the one before. The only change is in the horizontal axis where something has been done to experience the initial spike, which can be hard to manage just prior to start of game. How can you do this?

"The person I fear the most … is myself." -Tom Watson

The first step is to fully execute your pre-round and warm-up as discussed earlier. If you commit to filling up your EQ tank in the days leading up to game day and having all the items checked off, your anxiety spike will be lower than if you run to the first tee knowing there are things that you needed to do but did not get to.

The next step has to be done between 5 and 15 minutes prior to the first tee shot, not any sooner than that. Warming up before doing anything athletic is not a new strategy, but warming up with the specific purpose of spiking your heart rate intermittently just prior to doing something that you know will give you anxiety is something very different. Here are some induced activities you can do to get that heart rate spiked.

"I think that everything is possible as long as you put your mind to it and you put the work and time into it. I think your mind really controls everything." -Michael Phelps

Self-Inducing Initial HR Spike

The intention of these exercises is to purposefully get you to be out of breath (T level breathing).

1. Find an open space near or on the range and do some running suicide drills. These are very short and quick runs back and forth for just a few minutes. Take a very short break between to lower your heart, but quickly repeat. About 10 sets with only a 15 second burst of running will suffice in getting your HR up.
2. Do some jumping jack intervals. Very fast ones with arms and legs spread. Take a very short break between to lower your heart, but quickly repeat. About 10 sets with 10 jumping jacks with a 10 second rest will suffice in getting your HR up.
3. Line up 3 balls on the ground and hit each as fast and hard as possible with any club. Quickly set another 3 balls and do the same thing 10 times. This will also get your HR up.

During the brief break in these intervals, practice the breathing exercise with the intention of increasing your breathing counts (A level breathing) to slow your heart rate. While doing so, recall both your golf skill and EQ focal thoughts.

Though you may still be nervous and anxious once this is done as you get started to walk towards the first tee, you have tricked your body to lower levels of heart rate spikes, reducing the impact of the amygdala, and allowing you to access your memory for the all-important focal thoughts you need for that first swing and hole. You have essentially got the surprise of T level breathing out of the way before the first tee shot, instead of experiencing the HR spike at the first tee.

All of these recommendations should be practiced in your practice rounds and modified to make sure they are working for you.

Top 3 Ideas
I learned from this chapter
1.
2.
3.
3 Action Steps
I will take immediately to incorporate the above learning into my practice and taper days
1.
2.
3.

Chapter Summary

1. There are four parts to an effective warm up to a competitive round: EQ, Mental, Golf, and Physical.
2. A 90-minute warm-up time is recommended, broken into preparing for each of the four parts.
3. Practice potential mishaps before they occur during game day. For every potential mishap, have a possible solution prepared in your mind to help alleviate elevated levels of anxiety.
4. HR spikes are a symptom of anxiety and are always high at the beginning of the round on the first tee. You can trick your brain by simulating these spikes before the first tee so that it is lower on the first tee, which means lower cortisol and more access to your cognitive functions to make the right decision and golf skill on the first tee.

Chapter 7

When driving your car, you look at your speedometer to get a measurement of how fast or slow you are driving. It's a necessary gauge, and every car has it as the primary gauge in plain sight for the driver to see easily. If the gauge were not there, you would be guessing at your car's speed and not know when you were going above or below the speed limit. The speedometer helps you to perform within the established road speed limit. Similarly, I want you to consider adopting an EQ Speedometer – a gauge to help you monitor your emotional temperature. I've blogged about this before, sharing the Red, Yellow and Green levels in the Emotional Speedometer where GREEN is a calm state, RED is a very agitated state, and YELLOW is somewhere between the two where most of us operate.

The EQ Speedometer is depicted in the image attached. Imagine that this speedometer is with you at all times in every situation wherever you go. Before you start a meeting, or any activity, visualize this image and ask yourself where you are on the EQ Speedometer. Answer truthfully and know if your answer is YELLOW or RED, you are not going to perform at your best. Use the EQ Speedometer during your activity and use it on other people or for the environment you are in. Imagine this speedometer is in front of your eyes virtually all the time. Your strategy should be to get yourself, other people and the situation to GREEN if you want to optimize your chances of a great outcome.

This week, practice this. Use the speedometer as often as possible and especially before and during activities that require you to perform at a very high level. Not only will you FEEL better about your activities, but you are likely to also perform better.

https://izzyjustice.wordpress.com/2016/05/22/emotional-speedometer/

18 Holes of Competition

Practice	EQ & Mental Taper	Warm-up	Competitive Round	Goal Post	Refill EQ Tank	Practice

Figure 17. Phase: Competitive Round

Once the round has started, amidst the internal chaos, your first step is to use A level breathing to find your EQ focal thought. Find that happy and perfect memory from your cards. This will further reduce your HR as the thought will be comforting, and you know this because you have used items on the cards in training and it worked.

If you take your EQ temperature and note that your anxiety is still very high, then it is recommended you use your go-to tee shot - whatever that may be. Anything you know you can hit the ball into the fairway with the highest degree of comfort. A shot you can hit with your eyes closed. Perhaps it is a shot shape, a cut or a draw. It could be a trajectory shot, a low or high one. It could be a club, like a 3-wood or 5-wood. If you HR and anxiety is still high even after doing all the techniques recommended, then the go-to shot is the one to use.

During the round, recall that my definition of the most difficult shot to hit in golf is right after a bad one.

> **SCENARIO - First tee jitters:**
>
> I can remember the first opening tee shot that I hit in competition like it was yesterday, even though it was actually 26 years ago. You'd think that somewhere, in the thousands of tournament rounds between now and then, it would get easier, but it doesn't! However, some of the ways I've learned to cope with the jitters have made me more successful. If I'm in the middle or final rounds of a tournament, I take a few minutes and mentally replay the final few holes from the day before, remembering the intensity level I was feeling and getting a feel of the "flow" of the round. By doing that, the 1st tee today feels more like a continuation of yesterday's round. If I'm in the first round of a tournament, or even just playing a match against some friends, I will use my final few drives on the range to simulate the intensity level and consequence that my opening tee shot will have. The more successful I am at doing this on the range, the more comfort I feel when I stand over the ball on the first tee, because I feel like I've already done this today and it's not such a new or scary experience.
>
> -David Sanchez

Once the round has started, the following tools should be considered as important: 15th, 16th, 17th and 18th clubs; and used in the same way you would use a club in your bag. You use clubs in your bag based on the golf shot that needs to be executed. These tools should be used based on the emotional condition that you are in before and after each shot. You can determine your emotional state by taking your emotional temperature every five minutes by asking the simple question: How do I feel? The answer can be one of three: Green, Yellow or Red. These additional tools or 'clubs' are:

a) 15th Club: ACT Breathing Technique
b) 16th Club: EQ (mantra), Golf focal thoughts and Mental (course) strategy

c) 17th Club: Macro and Micro Focus using five senses for being present
d) 18th Club: Yellow and Red cards

These additional 'clubs' will take your club count to 18, just like the number of holes on the course. This will make it easy for you to remember. Note that the 16th and 18th clubs are written material that you can put in your yardage book, whereas the 15th and 17th clubs are skills you have learned earlier in this book that you will put into play when needed.

"It isn't the mountains ahead to climb that wear you out; it's the pebble in your shoe." -Muhammad Ali

---

SCENARIO - Poor start to round:

My opening few holes in a recent tournament could not have gone less smoothly. After hitting a poor opening tee shot, I followed it up with a second shot that was so unexpectedly off line that it made my jaw drop. The next few holes were equally shaky and when I reached the fourth green, I knew that I was dangerously close to the point where the rest of the round could become a disaster. The green on that particular hole was situated on the edge of a big, beautiful lake, so I decided to just turn my thoughts off and instead take as much of the scenery in as possible in the five minutes leading up to my next shot. Between the sight of the water, the sound of the birds in the trees, and the feel of the breeze, coupled with two sets of breathing in and out for 30 counts each, I stood over my next shot feeling like I had just been on a vacation and was totally relaxed. I made my putt for birdie and went on to play my strongest tournament of the year, winning by 5 shots.

-David Sanchez

Potential Round Mishaps

As in the previous chapter, it is worth making a list of all the mishaps that could potentially happen during your round. Here are some common ones:

1. Out of bounds shot.
2. Being outdriven by competitor.
3. Forgetting your hydration and nutrition.
4. Unexpected winds.
5. Duped into keeping pace with other players; abandoning your strategy.
6. Forgetting to eat and drink.
7. Bad lie.
8. Getting stung by a bee.
9. Rain.
10. A good shot that ends up in a bad spot.

This is a good point to review the examples given in Chapter 1 before proceeding with the exercise below. This is about how the new 18 clubs would have helped the players described in that chapter with their specific situations.

Make a list of 10 common mishaps that could happen to you in your round. For each one, think of a solution that includes all 18 clubs. Then, during practice, purposefully induce one or more of these mishaps and see if your solution would work.

1. Mishap:

   Solution:

2. Mishap:

   Solution:

3. Mishap:

   Solution:

4. Mishap:

   Solution:

5. Mishap: _____
_____

Solution: _____
_____
_____

6. Mishap: _____
_____

Solution: _____
_____
_____

7. Mishap: _____
_____

Solution: _____
_____
_____

8. Mishap: _____
_____

Solution: _____
_____
_____

9. Mishap: _____
_____

Solution: _____
_____
_____

> **10. Mishap:** _____
>
> **Solution:** _____

"I had to take a couple of deep breaths on the 17th after we squared the match because emotions were so high." -Sergio Garcia, 2016 Ryder Cup

The general strategy for the round should be:

1. Take your EQ temperature every five minutes. A vibrating alarm on your watch is a good idea. Be truthful with your answer to yourself knowing that once the round has started, you are likely going to underestimate your answer.
2. If your temperature is Yellow, then consider the shot you have to hit next, whatever it is, and find the corresponding Yellow card shot. For example, if you hit a shot poorly and you now have a 6-iron to hit on your next shot, then find the 6-iron shot on your yellow card. This should be your most recent perfect 6-iron, and that is the memory you want to have in your mind as you walk up to hit the next shot. You need this neuropathway to know you have used that tool (6-iron) before perfectly.
3. Practice Macro Focus in between shots and Micro Focus when over the ball on every shot. No exceptions. Catch yourself when your mind wanders and is thinking about anything but golf. A great measure to give yourself during/after the round is how many times you caught your mind wandering – thinking about anything other than golf.

4. At all times your breathing should be at A (abdomen) level around 15-20 counts in. Golf is not a high intensity sport and that should be taken advantage of. You can combine the A breathing with your round EQ mantra. Repeat the mantra in your mind with your breathing.
5. If the most important shot or shots to execute during the round are the ones after a bad one, then your reaction to that bad shot is the most critical skill to employ. After a bad shot:
    a) Breathe first to lower your heart rate. This will begin to lower cortisol.
    b) Use the Learning Template and assess whether the issue was golf related, EQ related or Mental (IQ) related. This is important to do so that the learning, which is positive, can quickly substitute for the negative experience. Learning from a negative will also lower cortisol level because you have found a positive in the mishap.
    c) Your walk to the next shot should be at your yellow card if it was not a major mishap. If it was a major mishap, then use the red card. Practice macro focus as much as you can. You must be in full green mode before you get to your next shot.
    d) Look at your yellow card a final time, and practice a deep micro focus for the next shot. Your emotions and thoughts should be on executing this shot to the best of your ability.

> **SCENARIO - Annoying playing partner:**
>
> As much as I try to like and enjoy everyone that I play each round with, the reality is that it doesn't always happen. Whether it's the way overly chatty person, the player who tries to get in your head, or the incredibly slow golfer, I have had to come up with a way to effectively keep my mind on my own game. The trick that has helped me the most over the years is to give myself little "jobs" to do to keep my mind occupied in between shots, so in other words, to macro focus. Instead of engaging in constant chatter or impatiently waiting and waiting for someone to hit their shot, I will repair stray divots in the fairways, improve on a less than perfect rake job in a bunker, or find a few unrepaired ball marks on the greens to fix. Before I know it, it is my turn to hit my shot again AND my EQ has gotten a boost because I found a way to improve the condition of the course that I was playing.
>
> -David Sanchez

The definition of Emotional Strength is the time it takes to convert a negative experience to a positive one – to go from yellow/red to green. Your ability to do this over and over again (since golf is a game of mishaps, which will get better the more you incorporate this into your repertoire), is a great measure of how truly emotionally strong you are. Conversely, the presence of negative monologues from negative conscious and subconscious memories should also indicate that you have a great deal of work to do in building emotional strength.

Additional EQ Strategy for Negative Monologues

One of the common issues golfers face is negative self-talk, monologues. Since golf is a game of mishaps, many golfers complain about the abusive language and negativity they use on themselves.

"There is no room in your mind for negative thoughts. The busier you keep yourself with the particulars of shot assessment and execution, the less chance your mind has to dwell on the emotional." –Jack Nicklaus

In addition to the strategy discussed in previous chapters, another EQ strategy is to prepare positive monologues to counteract these instinctive negative monologues. It really is quite simple. This was discussed in Chapter 2.

Pick experiences from your past that were very positive. It might be the story of when you graduated high school or college, a family vacation, helping someone else, an accomplishment, and such. These are stories, monologues, you can tell yourself and sometimes think about when describing 'good times' you had in your past.

Anytime you find your mind wandering, or going to a negative place, and having difficulty in macro or micro focus, then have these memories written out on a GREEN CARD and pull it out of your pocket and relive them. They are your 'good times' and a powerful tool for you. You can create 1-2 stories to use per holes as recommended below. Save the best positive for the last six holes, the next best ones for holes 6-12, and common ones for holes 1-6. Have these prepared in advance. And they should be changed up continuously the way you may change songs on a music playlist so that they are having the desired positive impact.

This same EQ Strategy is used very successfully by marathoners. For each of the 26 miles of the marathon, they find one person in their life to dedicate each mile to, or a powerful positive experience to think about, with the best ones saved for the latter stages of the marathon when fatigue and self-doubt really set in.

Round Monologue Strategy
Green Card

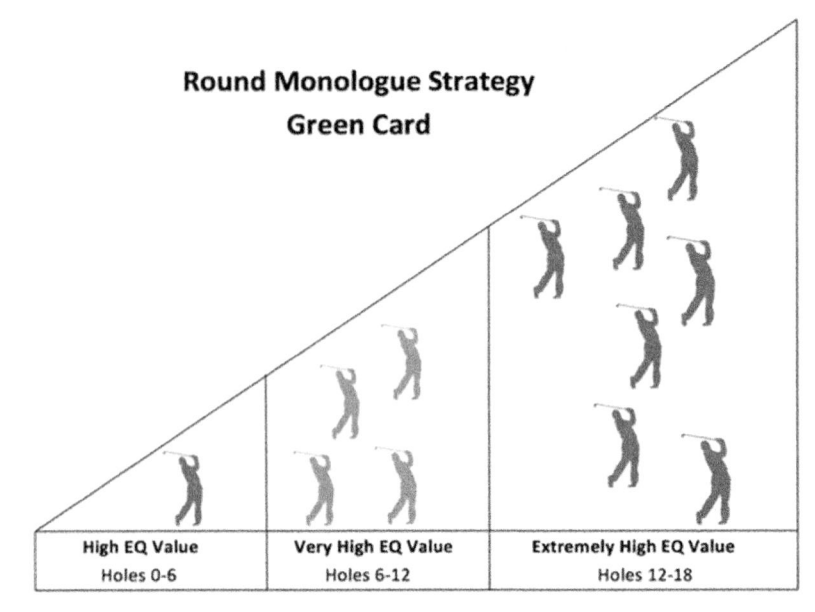

High EQ Value	Very High EQ Value	Extremely High EQ Value
Holes 0-6	Holes 6-12	Holes 12-18

Figure 18. Monologue Strategy

To be more specific, see the action items listed below for each three segments for the 18 holes.

<u>Holes</u>   <u>EQ Action Item</u>

0 - 6   Have your list of selected positive monologues playlist ready either on a card, or written on your yardage book. Write the 'headline' only of the story on each hole of the yardage book that you want for that hole. These stories are 'light' in nature and must be 100% positive in your narration. Good times!

6 - 12   Fill up your EQ tank with positive memories and monologues that are a little more meaningful. Use them especially if negative monologues begin to become louder and pervasive.

12 – 18   These are the best of the best stories of your life. They are bound to make you smile. Similar to the red card, but different in that the red card is to be used specifically when your EQ temperature is Red. These stories are to be used to keep the dopamine levels high to minimize cortisol spikes in those last important holes to finish strong.

> **SCENARIO - In the midst of a career round:**
>
> One of the goals on my "golf bucket list" has always been to break 60. While playing at my home course this summer, I made a long putt for eagle on the 14th hole that brought my goal within reach if I could birdie the last four holes. As the thought entered my mind, I felt the rush of chemicals through my body and immediately knew that managing my emotions would be absolutely critical from that point on. I made the conscious decision to enjoy the experience of the last four holes as much as possible, regardless of the outcome. I quickly adopted a new EQ mantra for those holes, which was simply, "I'm going for it!" After birdies on the next three holes, my goal was one more good hole away. I took in the whole moment and enjoyed it as much as possible. On the final green, I had a 15 footer to shoot 59. After some deep breathing and one last look at the surrounding scenery, I hit a great putt that just slid by the right edge, but didn't drop. The disappointment of coming up one shot shy was quickly replaced by my pride in the fact that I had not beaten myself and still shot a new career low round.
>
> -David Sanchez

You must believe that golf is as much a test of your physical abilities as it is your emotional strength. Both are being tested and at no greater point than when your negative self-talk begins to take fold especially after bad shots.

Take a look at your story in Chapter 1 where you underperformed. Could a golf, EQ and mental strategy like this have helped you?

For your next round create your own positive monologue play list for each hole to specifically manage negative self-talk.

Hole #	Positive Story
1.	_____
2.	_____
3.	_____
4.	_____
5.	_____
6.	_____
7.	_____
8.	_____
9.	_____
10.	_____
11.	_____
12.	_____
13.	_____
14.	_____
15.	_____
16.	_____
17.	_____
18.	_____

Nutrition/Hydration Strategy

Your body is burning calories and dehydrating when you are outside. You are depleting your body storage of glycogen and fueling becomes another key part of the round. It takes discipline, to consume what you need to at the time you need it. Your nutrition and hydration strategy comes from your training, and is unique to you. Working with a nutritionist to figure out the right foods and hydration for you is highly recommended as no amount of EQ, IQ or golf skill can compensate for an under-fueled physical body.

ReFuel Your EQ Tank

Your nutrition is not the only thing being depleted as the round progresses. On the course, your five senses are exposed to much more stimuli that can be used to your advantage. You are with fellow players, caddies, perhaps some fans, beautiful homes on the course, and all the sounds and smells that come with them. Each one can be a powerful refueling stimulus for your emotional energy that you have rapidly been depleting as you work to stay focused for 18 holes. As your body and mind begins to fatigue on the back nine, you are also depleting your EQ that you need for all the breathing, focal thoughts, and positive monologues.

One golfer has an EQ Focal Thought of saying "thank you" or "great shot" or any compliment he could think of to anyone around and even his fellow golfers. He counted every time he did it. He made sure that when he said thank you, he also smiled. He found that in return almost always, he was offered a compliment back which he found filled his EQ tank. His positive attitude, he contended afterwards, was the glue to his 18 holes. No matter what happened, he forced himself to find something about someone to compliment. This - neurologically - was a powerful way to fight his only true enemy on the course – his cortisol level.

"To control your nerves, you must have a positive thought in your mind." -Byron Nelson

Top 3 Ideas
I learned from this chapter
1.
2.
3.
3 Action Steps
I will take immediately to incorporate the above learning into my practice and taper days
1.
2.
3.

Chapter Summary

1. Begin to adopt 18 clubs in your bag, each to use for specific situations. The additional four clubs are a combination of all the items learned in previous chapters.
2. The hardest shot to hit is the one right after a bad one. This requires a very disciplined approach. Your ability to get to green before the next shot is your emotional strength.
3. Preparing for round mishaps is key to successfully navigating the game mishaps.
4. There are many ways to refuel your EQ Tank during the round and keep the dopamine levels high.

Chapter 8

When I ask anyone if they are smarter now than they were five years ago, the answer is always "yes!" I am told that the reason is that in the past five years, via all kinds of life experiences and training, they have learned a great deal. Alrighty then. Where do you store all that you have learned – not just in the past five years, but the past 10 or 20 years? If your answer to this question is "my brain" – then know that you have greatly diluted the value of the very experiences and learning you have earned.

I was sitting in the office of a senior executive sharing a solution to a challenging situation recently. He paused, got up and walked to a filing cabinet a few steps away, opened a drawer and shortly thereafter, pulled out a folder and showed it to me. "I went to a leadership training course in 2003 and most of what you just shared I had right here in my office all along. I just forgot." Even professional athletes "forget" to execute a plan that they spend weeks and months developing and training for. "I knew what to do – I just didn't do it," is a baffling comment many athletes share with their coaches. The reason for this is simple – they are all relying on the brain to (1) store the learning, and (2) to retrieve that learning at the most critical points when important decisions have to be made. The fact is that the brain is not a good place to store your life's learning. Here is why.

The brain has no taxonomy on how experiences should be stored except for a very high premium placed on storing negative experiences. The premium is based on the primary requirement of survival and our brain's design to alert us subconsciously to avoid similar negative experiences. The other reason is that unlike a filing cabinet or hard drive, the brain's ability to access learning and other knowledge changes constantly. Certain situations (calm, peaceful) allow us full access to all of them and others (fear, stress) in fact slow down or shut off entirely that access. The third reason is that good old fashioned rust (forgetfulness) – we do not frequent these learning nearly often enough to establish a roadway (neuropathway) to them to use when we most need them. Finally, what I call "white noise" – too many irrelevant experiences and "junk files" of life that get in the way to access those important learning.

The solution is not to substitute the brain (like an external drive) but to complement the brain by documenting learning elsewhere (stimulants) and then frequenting both the brain and the stimulant regularly. It is infinitely easier to do that today. You can create folders on mobile devices – folders for each dimension of your life. Spouse, Children, Leadership, Golf, Faith, Athlete, Swimming, Giving Feedback, and so on. This is your playbook to call the plays you need to execute in life that are based on your own personal life's experiences. As we approach this holiday season, I recommend you find a way that works best with your lifestyle and create this complementary storage that can help you trigger the right experiences/knowledge at the time you need it the most. Every time you learn something, or have an "aha" moment, capture it in this other storage mechanism. Imagine going through this after a full year. Not only will you amaze yourself, and likely have an outline of your personal memoir, but most importantly, you reduce duplication of the same mistakes the following year … and that's a character attribute of all great people.

https://izzyjustice.wordpress.com/2014/11/10/where-do-you-store-your-learning/

Post-Round

Practice	EQ & Mental Taper	Warm-up	Competitive Round	Goal Post	Refill EQ Tank	Practice

Figure 19. Phase: Post-Round

There are two key post-round functions to perform to continue to build your skills of learning and recovery.

Goal Post Model

You now know how to do this. Learning is best when done as close to the experience as possible. Within an hour of completing your round, and for sure before you leave the golf course, you should complete this model. This includes:

1. What you did well
2. What you need to work on
3. EQ evaluation
4. Golf evaluation
5. Mental evaluation

Processing your round this way to accurately measure how you did is a very healthy and productive piece of growth. All other sports do this in real time as coaches and athletes use this information for future practice. Re-read Chapter 3 if you need to at this point.

Potential Post-Round Mishaps

As in the previous chapter, it is worth making a list of all the mishaps that could potentially happen after your round. Here are some common ones:

1. Incorrect calculation of score.
2. Forget to turn in score card.
3. Forget to sign score card.
4. Blisters.
5. Indigestion.
6. Feeling sunburn.
7. Heavy wet shoes/clothes from rain.
8. Lose a club.

9. Message from loved one requiring your immediate attention.
10. Realized after turning card in that you broke a rule.

Even though the round of golf is over, mishaps after the round can be devastating emotionally and exacerbate cortisol levels to the detriment of how you sleep that night and your next round, especially if it is the next day.

> Make a list of 10 common mishaps that could happen to you after your round. For each one, think of a solution that includes all skills you have now learned. Then, if possible during practice, purposefully induce one or more of these mishaps and see if your solution would work.

> If any of these occur, the same technique of breathing and EQ management should be used to make sure a negative memory is not created and the mishap is handled appropriately.
>
> 1. Mishap:_____
> _____
>
>   Solution:_____
> _____
> _____
>
> 2. Mishap:_____
> _____
>
>   Solution:_____
> _____
> _____

3. Mishap: _____
   _____

   Solution: _____
   _____
   _____

4. Mishap: _____
   _____

   Solution: _____
   _____
   _____

5. Mishap: _____
   _____

   Solution: _____
   _____
   _____

6. Mishap: _____
   _____

   Solution: _____
   _____
   _____

7. Mishap: _____

   Solution: _____

8. Mishap: _____

   Solution: _____

9. Mishap: _____

   Solution: _____

10. Mishap: _____

   Solution: _____

What not to do post-round

Contrary to what many do, from a neuroscience perspective, there are a few activities not recommended post-round. The primary reason is that if you just played a round using all the golf, EQ and mental skills you have learned, then your neuropathways are not ready to effectively learn or imprint anything new. Fatigue of all kinds, mental, emotional and physical, will be high and your stress hormones will be fully engaged working to get you to rest or shut down. This is cortisol family at work. At least four hours of rest and recovery should occur before considering doing any of these activities so that other hormones (from recovery experiences) can dilute the cortisol levels. Here are some common post-round activities to avoid:

1. Going to the range.
2. Working specifically on your mishaps.
3. Negative self-talk.
4. Negative talking to others about their rounds.
5. Alcohol consumption.
6. Heavy or unhealthy meals.
7. Forget to eat/drink.
8. Forget to process goal post learning.

Recovery

Given you are being told what not to do, what should you be doing in addition to the goal post learning after your round? During your round, you have actively used many skills. Physical(walking 18 holes), mental, and emotional. The physiology of the mind is no different than that of any other muscle where, when used, it needs to recover to perform well subsequently.

"The man who views the world at 50 the same as he did at 20 has wasted 30 years of his life." –Muhammed Ali

A more important question to ask is why recovery is not given the same consideration as practicing on the range or playing a round? One answer is that recovery does not result in fatigue and tangible result like a score (two feel-good outcomes of playing) and therefore, we assume it is of no benefit. Related to this is the lack of the endorphin high (experienced during rounds) that may hinder you from fully recovering.

In addition, most of us think of recovery as just something that will happen naturally by itself when you are not playing or hitting balls.

Advantages of Recovery

1. Allow for body to physically recover.
2. Allow dopamine levels to dilute cortisol levels.
3. Time needed to re-direct neuropathways (thinking) from 'heat of the moment' ones (fast) to more rational and slower mode.
4. Allow body to prepare for future activity.
5. Better sleep.
6. Prevent injury.
7. Reduce emotional stress (allowing for refilling of EQ Tank).
8. Removal of metabolic waste.
9. Prevent burn out.
10. Restore balance and reduce overload.

Active Recovery

Active recovery is a wonderful way to incorporate the benefits of recovery while still being active. You are still doing something, but doing so at a very low intensity. Active recovery is strongly recommended in between rounds. Examples of active recovery are listed below; but keep in mind that an attribute of active recovery is your ability to be mostly at A level breathing:

1. Low intensity swim.
2. Short HR Zone 1 run or bike.
3. Yoga or Pilates.
4. Core or stretch workout.
5. Massage.
6. Short power nap.
7. Closing of eyes and engaging in other senses than sight.
8. Walk.

9. Ice Bath.
10. Re-filling up your EQ Tank (same as taper days).

Re-filling your EQ tank is one of the more important emotional strength building recovery activities you can do. If you have another competitive round the next day, then you are limited with what you can do, but it becomes even more important to do. It was already recommended to fill up your EQ tank for 1-3 days before this round, and now you have less than a day to do so before your next round. All the activities described for your taper days should be considered for your evening and early morning time before your next round. Include some of the active recovery exercises above. You will find yourself more 'fresh' the next day, which is a layman's term for describing dilution of cortisol and a break for your neuropathways. Without this recovery, and EQ refill, your progressive rounds will be even more challenging from an EQ and Mental perspective.

Sleep

Sleep is another key part of recovery. Studies indicate that an average athlete needs about 8-9 hours of quality sleep a day. Consider that most golfers have competing obligations, it is common to cut into this required sleep time for recovery. If this resonates with you, then mastering the skill of sleeping itself is a key competency for you as a golfer. Again, it will require emotional competence, not physical, to orchestrate a sleep strategy.

Some professional golfers are notoriously protective of their sleep. When traveling, many are known to take their own beds, pillows and other personalized sleep essentials with them on the road. They have also figured out a go-to-sleep routine that works for them. For many, it means going to bed earlier, cutting off all electronics several hours before intended sleep time to avoid keeping-me-awake thoughts. It also means not having any caffeine, sugars or any other type of food that will compromise their sleep. I also encourage athletes to take their EQ temperature as they begin their sleep routine and use the YELLOW card in the same manner as in competition to address any negative monologues so that they can be substituted with positive ones that would allow them to sleep.

As golfers, you are encouraged to measure your sleep during your golf season and embrace a sleep routine much like the professionals do.

Sleep and active recovery are also essential to your EQ. There is a finite amount of emotional energy you have each day and it needs to be spread around all of life's activities, not just your golf. Recovery and active recovery are both excellent times to refuel your EQ tank.

"Sleep is the best meditation". -Dalai Lama

Build Your Recovery Plan

> *From the list of active recovery activities, pick 5 that you feel you can integrate immediately into your routine.*
>
> 1. _____
>
> 2. _____
>
> 3. _____
>
> 4. _____
>
> 5. _____

> *Write down your current go-to-sleep routine, if you have one.*
> _____
> _____
> _____

> *Write down modifications to your sleep routine so that you can ensure 8-9 hours of quality sleep.*
> _____
> _____
> _____

Nutrition/Hydration Strategy

As recommended earlier, an appointment with a sport nutritionist is highly recommended. There are certain types of food and hydration that work very well with recovery. You will have to figure this out based on your physiology. Generally speaking, a clean meal with proteins like fish, vegetables and light carbohydrates are better post-activity. What might be more valuable to you is to share with the nutritionist what you currently do and what you may need to replace, reduce, or cut out entirely.

Top 3 Ideas
I learned from this chapter
1.
2.
3.

3 Action Steps
I will take immediately to incorporate the above learning into my post-round strategy
1.
2.
3.

Chapter Summary

1. What you do after a round is critical to building your emotional strength for subsequent rounds. The two key areas are goal post learning and recovery.
2. Refilling your EQ tank is a critical step of recovery.
3. Active recovery is a powerful way to give your body the necessary break it needs to recover.

Chapter 9

On a recent business trip, I reconnected with a dear friend whom I had not seen in several years. She told me she had ended her personal relationship and was single again. About a year ago, she joined a group of single women mostly over the age of 50 who met once a month for an experience. The purpose of the experience was to literally experience something new and different that would somehow enrich their lives, their understanding of life, and expand their horizons. These were not 'bucket list' type of experiences. They were perhaps just one tier below that. For example, the previous week, one of the ladies arranged for tickets to hear a very well-known author who was on a book tour promoting his new book. They also arranged to meet with him afterwards for a private Q&A. None of them had ever done anything like this before, but all of them found it a very powerful new experience. As I listened to my friend, I was incredibly impressed and began to wonder why this wonderful concept could not be stolen and applied to married couples, couples in a relationship, a family goal, and best of all, at work within a team.

This week, whether you are an officially designated leader at work or not, I invite you to present this idea to your team as a goal for 2013. Your team should have an experience a month with the same purpose of enriching each other's lives through the experience. Depending on the size of the team, make one or more people responsible for each month. I encourage you to do so during work hours to guarantee attendance. Please note that a team lunch, bowling, or other traditional activities often designated as 'team building' ones do not count. The once-a-month experiences have to be something that most of your team have not experienced before. I would love to be a fly on the wall at your experiences, or better yet, observe your team the day after.

https://izzyjustice.wordpress.com/2013/01/20/an-experience-a-month/

Caddying

This role does not apply to many golfers as the overwhelming majority will not have a caddy when playing golf. However, other folks often will play this role. It might be a parent, a sibling, a friend, a coach, or a professional caddie. If you play one of these roles, being a caddie for someone else, then this chapter is for you. If you are a player who uses a caddie, then you may want to offer this book to them so the two of you are aware of the new 18 clubs and techniques.

As a caddie, you are in a very enviable position to have a huge impact on your golfer. Anyone can clean balls, clubs, get yardages, and rake bunkers, but a good caddie is a trusted confidant and for all practical purposes, the perfect person to be a sports psychologist for the golfer. A caddie can say one word, like that EQ mantra, or do one thing, like show a smile, that can quickly change the emotional temperature of the player. On the other hand, and perhaps inadvertently, a caddie can also say or do the wrong thing that can get the golfer to yellow or red. So awareness of the tools in this book can be invaluable.

As a caddie, your first order of business is to complete this book. Then give it to your player and have it completed by them. Read each other's books and responses to all the exercises. Have a discussion about your responses. You will learn an enormous amount about each other beyond the game of golf that you can apply immediately in your next round.

Practice those breathing techniques yourself – you, too, need to be in green. Know what is in your player's yellow and red cards. Explore the focusing techniques. Take each other's emotional temperature and guess whether you are right or wrong. Agree to what parts of the golf, EQ, and mental strategies you, as the caddie, can play.

Consider the sequence below.

Practice	EQ & Mental Taper	Warm-up	Competitive Round	Goal Post	Refill EQ Tank	Practice

Figure 20. Review Phases for Caddy

A good caddie should make sure that a good taper is done, when the EQ Tank is loaded. You should also know what the EQ and mental strategy is so that you are on the same page, but more importantly, you can re-direct once off the strategy by using the same techniques.

A good caddie should also hold the player disciplined to the warm-up routine and make sure all the phases in the 90-minute session are done correctly.

You should monitor your player's emotional temperature when ready to go to the first tee. If it is yellow or red, practice your anxiety inducing jumping jacks or something similar. Do it together. Have fun with it.

"There is no room on the golf course for anger or self-pity." –Greg Norman

When playing your round of golf, your most important role will be to keep your player as green as possible from the first tee shot till the last putt on 18. All the techniques of breathing, macro and micro focus, mantras, and managing the monologues should be used. The good news is that the monologues will be dialogues since you can talk to them. You can quickly assess the positivity or negativity of the dialogue. You can insert a positive dialogue – one that you previously agreed to while sharing your strategy.

Make sure the post-round activities are done. You can be a part of the recovery process also, as you too will be tired from all your work carrying the bag.

As a caddie, you can see how impactful you can be to the success of your player.

> **SCENARIO - Parenting/Caddying/Coaching:**
>
> A player, whether they realize it or not, takes on the added role of wanting to satisfy the other parts of their "team", and this extra piece of responsibility is often a burden that makes performing well too much to handle if the other team member doesn't give the player the tools necessary for them to succeed.
>
> A parent/caddie/coach's primary responsibility is to make sure that they are in Green THEMSELVES. A player can instantly pick up on gestures and body language that suggest that another member of their team is in Red or Yellow. Anything like constant pacing, jingling change or keys in their pockets, constantly smoking, speaking quickly, or being very indecisive or uncertain about simple decisions can give off the strong sense of someone experiencing high levels of anxiety and are likely to carry over to the player as well.
>
> The strongest way to put a player in Yellow or Red is by making the wrong comment or gesture after a poor shot. I have heard too many to count, but some very common ones are:
>
> "What were you thinking on that one???"
> "You weren't even trying on that one!!!"
> "I haven't seen you hit one that bad in years!!!"
> "You should just quit if you're going to play like this!"
> "This is such a waste of my time to come out and have you play like this!"

"I can't believe that I spent all that money on you to play golf!"
"You're such a disappointment to me!"

Even without saying anything, there is also the negative body language of the caddie who angrily picks up the bag, throws it over his shoulder, and walks off way ahead of his player.

Solution:

1. Your response, verbal or non-verbal, to your player's shots, especially poor shots, will make your player even more yellow/red. Build strong awareness to how you are communicating by making sure it is more green-enabling than yellow/red enabling.
2. Breathe. Take A level breaths and use language or non-verbals that can take your player to green.
3. Remind your player to engage in green activities, such as positive dialogues and monologues, their cards, breathing, etc. Get them to green by all means necessary before the next shot.

-David Sanchez

From all that you have read, pick 10 changes that you feel you can integrate immediately as a caddie.

1. _____
2. _____
3. _____
4. _____
5. _____
6. _____
7. _____
8. _____
9. _____
10. _____

Top 3 Ideas

I learned from this chapter

1.
2.
3.

3 Action Steps

I will take immediately to help my player

1.
2.
3.

Chapter Summary

1. Being a caddie is an invaluable role for a golfer to have.
2. Both caddie and player should read this book, exchange each other's completed books, and learn about each other to become a better team.
3. A caddie should use the same tools to reinforce the importance of EQ by keeping his player green throughout the round.

Chapter 10

Last week, I offered a simple neurological definition of Happiness – the constant pursuit of eliminating fear in how we feel, think, and do. This week, let's discuss where and how fear manifests itself so that you can recognize those experiences both as they occur and preferably, before they occur. There are three distinctive scenarios for causality of fear: (1) those that we cause (2) those that others cause, and (3) those that a situation causes. Any of these causes by themselves can release significant levels of cortisol – the opposite of the happiness hormone. Any combination of these or worse, all 3 together, can result in debilitating trauma that can cause long term or even a permanent state of unhappiness, where no amount of happy moments can result in happiness. The absolute worst case scenario is when as a result of this, you, as an initial victim, now become a perpetrator and create a cycle of unhappiness. These are reasons to really understand just how powerful of a positive impact removal of fear can have on your life, happiness, and performance.

The ones that we cause are based on our own past experiences. Lay terms to describe this cause include "feeling insecure" or "not a risk-taker" or "lacking courage." There are many reasons for this state but the result is that you own this, and you are solely responsible for this. The second one is caused by others. In the workplace, it might be an abusive boss or peer. In athletics, in might be a competitor. In life, it might be a relative who brings out the worst in you. Make no mistake, in this scenario, though you are not causing it, you are without question complicit in it and an enabler. How so? The worse you feel about yourself (already high levels of cortisol), the easier it is for others to take advantage of you (increase those already-high cortisol levels). The last one is a situation. It might be a big meeting at work in front of key people or the last few miles in a marathon, the gravity (consequence) of the situation is so high that cortisol levels reach the same levels as though someone has pulled a gun on you at a grocery store. Totally different situations, but identical neurological reactions. You can understand now just how and why the experiences combining all three causes can be traumatic. For those in the business of high performance, whether you are a leader in a company or a competitive athlete, you must have fear-removing skills to having a fighting chance to be successful.

The first step in removing fear is to take inventory of these causes. Make three columns on paper with each of these causes: You, Others, Situations. Under each one, be honest and list specific (about three under each category) and recent experiences (past year) where you recognize the cause of your fear. For example, under Others, there might be a business meeting last week where someone did something that caused you to feel some anxiety or fear and make you be extra cautious. Once you make this list, can you find common attributes in all those experiences? Are you able to see a pattern of what it is that you are really afraid of – what causes fear to be present in your life? If you believe in the premise of last week's blog, that happiness is really about removing fear and if you can do this exercise this week, then you are now ready to pursue the removal of fear.

https://izzyjustice.wordpress.com/2015/02/22/happiness-part-2/

Life Balance

In this last chapter, I will take the happiness topic discussed in Chapter 4 to a very practical and holistic level.

Last checked, golfers are human beings. You are someone's son, daughter, mom, dad, spouse, and so on. These most important roles do not go away by being a golfer. This means you are responsible for all the things that come with being a father, mother, significant other, neighbor, friend, brother, sister, uncle, aunt, relative, co-worker, boss, and the like. The case has already been made regarding how 'you' happy will outperform 'you' unhappy.

Happy athletes tend to be more focused and have a balanced meaning to their sport, be able to find focus when it is not there, and perform more consistently at higher levels than those who are not happy.

The purpose of this chapter is to help you analyze your life so that you can have balance, and happiness as a result. There are several important exercises in this chapter that I ask you to take as seriously as all the other exercises I have asked you to do in the previous chapters.

"Crises are part of life. Everybody has to face them, and it doesn't make any difference what the crisis is." -Jack Nicklaus

Know what needs to be balanced

The first step in having a balance is to know what exactly it is that needs balancing. For some it may be spouse and kids, but for others it could be parents or other loved ones. Knowing what needs to be balanced will, in turn, make it clear for you to balance them.

Who are you?

No, this is not a philosophical question. In fact, it is a very pragmatic question. Each one of us has many a role to play in life.

In no prioritized order, please list the 10 most important roles you currently play (e.g., Son, brother, etc.):
1.
2.
3.

4.	
5.	
6.	
7.	
8.	
9.	
10.	

Your Circle of Life

In the chart below, and from the list above, take the top five most important roles you need to play in the next 12 months, and insert them into the circles around you.

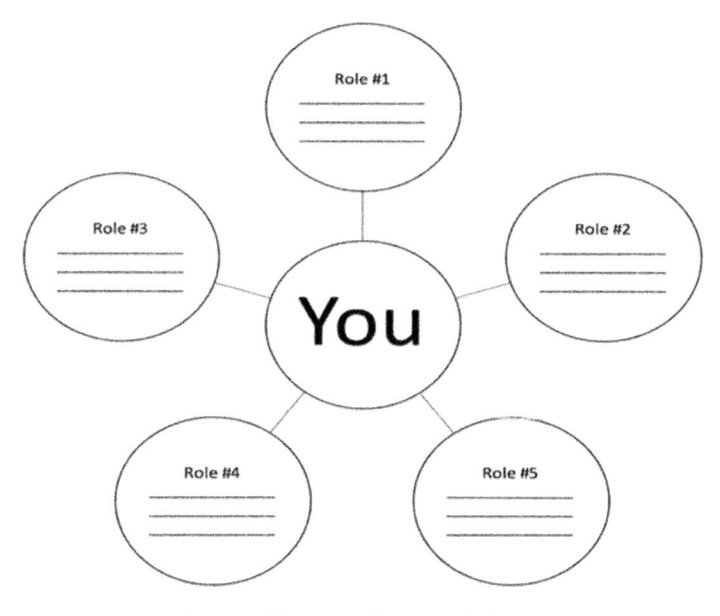

Figure 20. Your Circle of Life

This represents your EQ universe. These roles are so important to you that your performance in ALL of them will dictate your performance in EACH one of them. The emotional relationship, and therefore power, that each has to your emotional state cannot be underscored enough. A committed effort to keep all these green is, in fact, an effort to keep yourself green.

"Sports are a microcosm of society." -Billie Jean King

Empathy

In EQ, one of the core dimensions is empathy. Simply put, it is the ability to take someone else's emotional temperature. If you can look at people, at their behavior or language, and know whether they are green, yellow, or red, then you have very good empathy skills.

For the people that are in the five key roles you play, it is strongly recommended that you practice empathy with them all the time in much the same way you were asked to take your EQ temperature every five minutes when playing your competitive round. It is a very simple question: How is that person feeling right now? He or she can only be one of three: green, yellow or red. Having empathy and practicing empathy with the people in your key roles by itself is a powerful emotional strength builder for you as you will able to do it for yourself and, more importantly, you will enable those same people to do it to you when you are unable to do it for yourself.

Just as when you take your EQ temperature and the result is yellow or red, you now know how to get yourself to green. You breathe, use your cards and can practice the focus (mindfulness) techniques you have learned. For the people in the five key roles of your life, it is strongly recommended that you know their yellow and red cards. If you took your spouse's EQ temperature and it was yellow, for example, and you had prepared a yellow card of activities (best of) that you know will turn her back to green, then you are using emotional intelligence, not logic or rationale (IQ), which brings about happiness for you in that role. Taking all you have learned for yourself and your round of golf should easily translate to these key roles and dimensions of your life so that they can always be green too. This is happiness and balance in all dimensions of your life - and a key to your own personal performance when you go out to play golf.

On the contrary, the more yellow or red these roles are, or the people in them, the more challenging (unhappy) it will be for you to perform at a high level.

Monitor Your EQ Day

Up until now I have asked you to center your EQ strategy around golf. I have taught you how to transition from work or home life into golf life so that you can be focused. But according to your EQ Universe above, your being a golfer is only one part of your world – one fifth of your EQ tank. Daily or weekly, as you enter the other roles in your universe, roles that collectively will determine your happiness (GREEN state), you will need to execute the same EQ strategy described in previous chapters of measuring your EQ temperature and using the tools I have given you to make sure that before entering the other roles, you are in GREEN mode. Though these other roles are different in terms of logistics, time and skill requirement, they are identical in their EQ requirement of you being GREEN. In other words, emotionally, you have to perform at your best so that these other roles are not compromised. The five roles do not require an equal investment of time, but do require an equal investment of your emotional energy. If you are out of golf balls, as an example, you simply go to the store and buy more. You have done something to make the imbalance of being a golfer balanced. That same emotional commitment needs to be made if anything in your five roles needs fixing too.

Look at the graph below. On the vertical axis is your EQ Thermometer with GREEN being at the top. On the horizontal axis is the time of day sequenced in 3-hour increments.

Think of your day yesterday from the time you woke up till you went to bed. Think of where you were, what you were doing, and most importantly, how you felt at that time (GREEN, YELLOW or RED). At each 3-hour mark for the whole day yesterday, put an "X" on how you felt on the vertical axis, based on your EQ temperature.

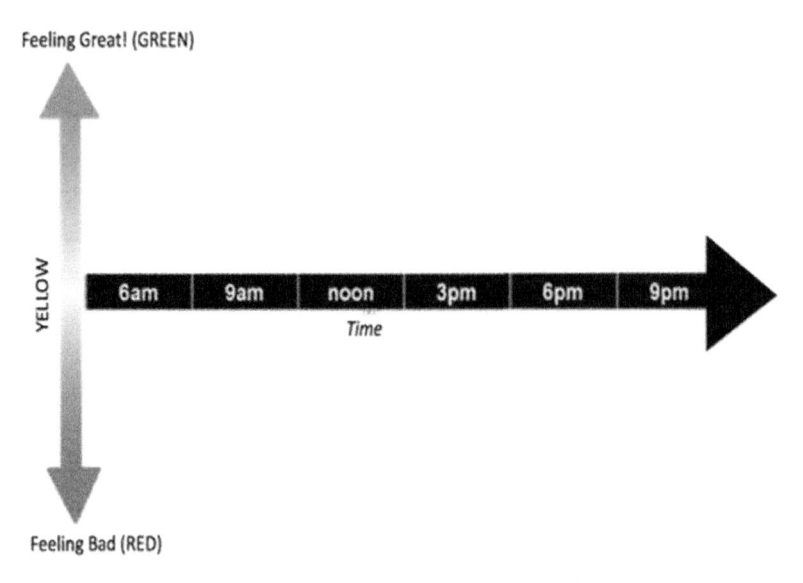

Figure 21. Monitoring EQ Temperature

For most people, there will be some highs and lows depending on how their day went. You can do this same exercise for the previous week, month, year, or past 10 or 20 years by just changing the units of the horizontal axis.

Note: It can be a very powerful tool to do this exercise for your entire life. Have your time line in increments of 5 years to your present age. Plot "X" to the points in your life that were high and low with a one-word descriptor for each one. Refer to the exercise you did in Chapter 2 for experiences in your negative memory bank. Once you do this, you may find a correlation between the events of your low points and the negative monologues you tend to have.

What is important to note is that each day you are likely to be in all colors. This is perfectly normal, and quite frankly, a sign of being emotionally healthy. But if you have to make an important decision, or have to have an important conversation, or be present for an important event for the other roles in your life, when do you think, based on your completed EQ graph of your day yesterday, would have been the best time to do this? Clearly, it would have been when you were GREEN. That is when, from a neuroscience perspective, you feel least threatened (low cortisol, high dopamine), and full uninhibited access to all your skills and memories – stuff that you will need to be at your best for the important conversation, decision or event.

This is a key point in having a balance in your life. Balance is not about quantity of time you spend in each role, but the quality of time. Knowing that as a golfer, a huge chunk of your time will be diverted to your sport, it is all the more important to monitor your EQ temperature day by day and make sure you are fully GREEN in the other roles, especially when important events in those roles need you to be.

"A man who dares to waste one hour of time has not discovered the value of life." -Charles Darwin

If you have had a bad day on the course, or a bad day in one of the roles, I do not recommend you "fake" being in GREEN and show up in your other roles with a fake smile, for example. Those that know you well will see right through it. What you need to do is to use your EQ strategy, in much the same way as you would if you hit a bad shot in your round and knowing now that how you respond to it is more important than the mishap itself, as described in the many examples in Chapter 1. In this context, a golf game is a wonderful metaphor of life itself. Golf is a game of mishaps much like life. There will be holes you will play very well, like times in your life when things are going well. There will be holes you will not play so well and be tested in your maturation, just like life will test you with hardships. And this just may be the allure of it all, and the answer to why golf is both one of the most loved sports, and why golfers chase that perfect round the same way we all chase that perfect life.

Life's Mishaps

In the next year, just as in a round, life too will have some mishaps. If they occur in any of the roles that are most important to you, then, just as in a round, have a plan for them.

> **Make a list of 10 life's mishaps that could happen to you in the next 12 months ONLY in the roles in your EQ universe. (Note – if mishaps happen outside of those roles, you do not need to list them here). For each one, think of a solution. Then, as part of making sure you have a balanced life optimizing your happiness, think through by discussing with people in those roles what your solution will be.**
>
> 1. Mishap: _____
>   _____
>
>   Solution: _____
>   _____
>   _____
>
> 2. Mishap: _____
>   _____
>
>   Solution: _____
>   _____
>   _____

3. Mishap: _____
_____

   Solution: _____
_____
_____

4. Mishap: _____
_____

   Solution: _____
_____
_____

5. Mishap: _____
_____

   Solution: _____
_____
_____

6. Mishap: _____
_____

   Solution: _____
_____
_____

7. Mishap: _____
_____

   Solution: _____
_____
_____

8. Mishap: _____

_____

Solution: _____

_____

_____

9. Mishap: _____

_____

Solution: _____

_____

_____

10. Mishap: _____

_____

Solution: _____

_____

_____

"Every man dies. Not every man really lives." -William Wallace

I hope that this book has been a journey of learning for you. One that takes the wonderful sport of golf and brings out the best in you. Training to be your best for your important round is the same as training to be your best in life. Now, what could be better?

Top 3 Ideas
I learned from this chapter
1.
2.
3.
3 Action Steps
I will take immediately to incorporate the above learning for a more balanced life
1.
2.
3.

Chapter Summary

1. Happy and balanced athletes tend to be more focused, be able to find focus when it is not there, and perform more consistently at higher levels than those who are not happy.
2. Take the time to properly analyze your life and situations so that you can achieve balance and happiness both in your personal life and golf life.
3. Just as in golf, life too will have some mishaps. If they occur in any of the roles with people in them that are most important to you, you now have a plan for them by practicing empathy and the same skills you will use in golf.

About the Author

Dr. Izzy Justice is a sports neuropsychologist and an avid golfer. He has worked with professional athletes, coaches, and teams in a myriad of sports. He was the first to formally introduce EQ to sports and is considered one of the pre-eminent experts in Emotional Intelligence, having published five books previously and in several sports magazines. He speaks globally on EQ and his weekly blog (http://izzyjustice.wordpress.com) is widely read. He and his family live on Lake Norman in North Carolina. This book was written in Eagles Nest in Banner Elk, NC.

Printed in Great Britain
by Amazon